About this book

This Practice Workbook contains questions to target every topic in Year 6 Maths.

Questions split into three levels of increasing difficulty – Challenge 1, Challenge 2 and Challenge 3 – to aid progress.

Symbols to highlight questions that test problem-solving skills.

Total marks boxes for each challenge and topic.

'How am I doing?' checks for self-evaluation.

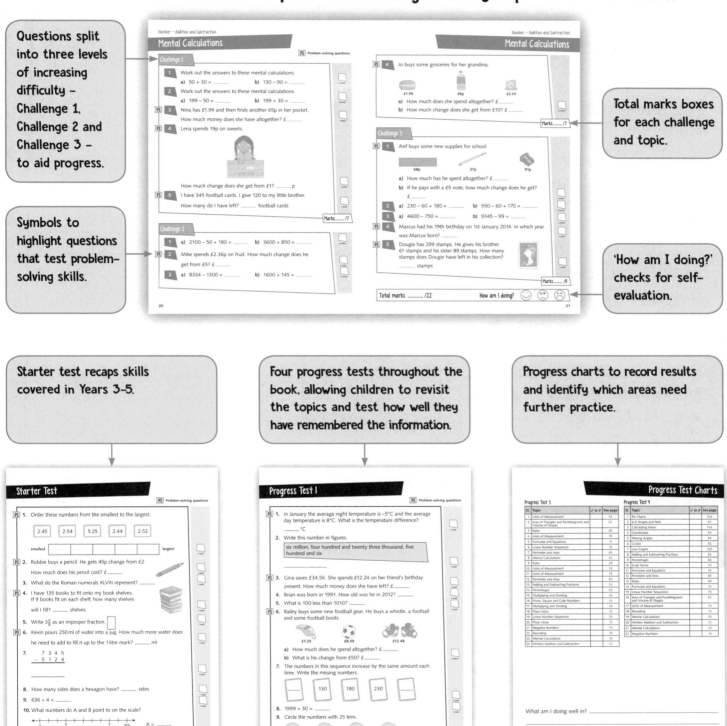

Starter test recaps skills covered in Years 3–5.

Four progress tests throughout the book, allowing children to revisit the topics and test how well they have remembered the information.

Progress charts to record results and identify which areas need further practice.

Answers for all the questions are included in a pull-out answer section at the back of the book.

Author: Frances Naismith

Contents

Contents

ACKNOWLEDGEMENTS

The author and publisher are grateful to the copyright holders for permission to use quoted materials and images.

p28 © Hemera/Thinkstock
p44 © Shutterstock.com/IreneArt

Every effort has been made to trace copyright holders and obtain their permission for the use of copyright material. The author and publisher will gladly receive information enabling them to rectify any error or omission in subsequent editions. All facts are correct at time of going to press.

Published by Collins

An imprint of HarperCollins*Publishers*
1 London Bridge Street
London SE1 9GF

© HarperCollins*Publishers* Limited 2015

ISBN 9780008175498

First published 2015

14

All rights reserved. No part of this publication may be reproduced, stored in a retrieval system, or transmitted, in any form or by any means, electronic, mechanical, photocopying, recording or otherwise, without the prior permission of Collins.

British Library Cataloguing in Publication Data.

A CIP record of this book is available from the British Library.

Series Concept and Development: Michelle I'Anson
Commissioning and Series Editor: Chantal Addy
Author: Frances Naismith
Project Manager and Editorial: Rebecca Rothwell
Cover Design: Sarah Duxbury and Paul Oates
Inside Concept Design: Ian Wrigley
Text Design and Layout: Contentra Technologies
Artwork: Collins and Contentra Technologies
Production: Niccolò de Bianchi
Printed in Great Britain by Martins the Printers

PS **1.** Order these numbers from the smallest to the largest.

| 2.45 | 2.54 | 5.25 | 2.44 | 2.52 |

smallest | | | | | | largest

1 mark

PS **2.** Robbie buys a pencil. He gets 45p change from £2.

How much does his pencil cost? £_____

1 mark

3. What do the Roman numerals XLVIII represent? _____

1 mark

PS **4.** I have 135 books to fit onto my book shelves.
If 9 books fit on each shelf, how many shelves

will I fill? _____ shelves

1 mark

5. Write $3\frac{5}{8}$ as an improper fraction. ☐

1 mark

PS **6.** Kevin pours 250 ml of water into a jug. How much more water does

he need to add to fill it up to the 1 litre mark? _____ ml

1 mark

7.
```
    7 3 4 5
  – 5 1 2 4
  _____
```

1 mark

8. How many sides does a hexagon have? _____ sides

9. 636 ÷ 4 = _____

1 mark

10. What numbers do A and B point to on the scale?

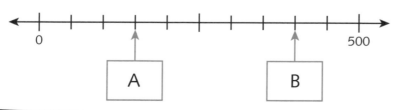

0   500

A = _____

B = _____

2 marks

PS **11.** Joe buys two pens and a ruler. The ruler costs £1.60
He gets £1.54 change from £5.00
How much did one pen cost? _____ p

12. Write this number in figures.

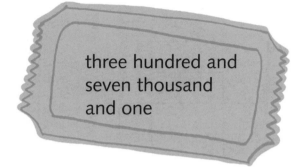

three hundred and
seven thousand
and one

_____

PS **13.** Computer tablets cost £230 each.
If a school wants to buy 15 new tablets,
how much will they have to spend?

£ _____

£230

14. What is $\frac{3}{8}$ of 128? _____

PS **15.** The cross-country team kept a record of the number of laps they ran
in training.

Name	Number of laps
Janet	45
Terry	63
Nikhil	27
Denise	31

a) Who ran the most laps? _____

b) How many laps did the team run altogether? _____ laps

c) How many more laps did Terry run than Nikhil? _____ laps

PS **16.** Brodie travels to school on the 7.45 am bus.
The journey takes 25 minutes. What time does

Brodie arrive at school? _____

5

17. Write $\frac{16}{3}$ as a mixed number.

1 mark

18. Round 5176 to the nearest:

   a) 10 _____   **b)** 100 _____   **c)** 1000 _____

3 marks

PS **19.** What 3-D shapes do these nets represent?

   a)   **b)**

_____   _____

2 marks

PS **20.** Sami and Lucy each buy a sandwich.
Sami gets 13p change from £1 and Lucy
gets £2.84 change from £5. How much did

their sandwiches cost altogether? £_____

1 mark

21. Order these fractions from smallest to largest.

$\frac{4}{6}$ $\frac{1}{2}$ $\frac{5}{12}$ $\frac{1}{4}$

smallest | | | | | largest

1 mark

PS **22.** The Smith family save up £57.93
They buy a new microwave costing £23.45
How much money do they have left over?

£_____

1 mark

23. Draw the lines of symmetry on this shape.

1 mark

24. If I turn round $1\frac{1}{2}$ times, how many degrees have I travelled

through? _____

1 mark

PS **25.** I come back from a fortnight's holiday on the 11th December.

On which date did I go away? _____

1 mark

26. Write these fractions as decimals.

a) $\frac{75}{100}$ _____

b) $\frac{3}{10}$ _____

c) $\frac{56}{1000}$ _____

3 marks

27. Circle the angles that are greater than 90°.

A   B   C   D

1 mark

PS **28.** The sports shop is having a sale.

25% off

How much will the trainers cost now?

£64.80

£_____

1 mark

PS **29.** Billy runs a race in $1\frac{1}{4}$ minutes. Peter takes 20 seconds longer.

How long does Peter take to run his race? _____ seconds

1 mark

PS **30.** I buy two highlighter pens and a notebook.
The notebook cost £2.20. I get £2.40 change from £10.

How much does each highlighter pen cost? £_____

1 mark

PS **31.** Mohammed thinks of a number. He subtracts 3 then doubles
his answer. He adds 4. The number he is left with is 18.

What was his starting number? _____

1 mark

32. What are all the factors of 32?

_____   _____   _____   _____   _____   _____

1 mark

PS **33.** Sura pours some flour onto her scales.
They read 156 g. How much more flour would
Sura need to add to make the scales read 1 kg?

_____ g

1 mark

34. Fill in the blanks to make the statement correct.

170 – _____ = 150 + _____

1 mark

PS **35.** Lucy is going to save £3.15 every week. How many weeks will she
need to save to afford a new phone cover costing £12.60?

_____ weeks

1 mark

36. Shade $\frac{1}{5}$ of this shape.

1 mark

37.   5 2 3 4
      + 4 3 7 6
      _____

      _____

1 mark

38. Circle the prime numbers.

3   25   31   42   51   67   75

1 mark

39. Fill in the missing numbers

    a) $33 \div 10 =$ _____

    b) $130 \div$ _____ $= 1.3$

    c) _____ $\div 100 = 0.33$

3 marks

40. a) $3^3 =$ _____

    b) $12^2 =$ _____

    c) $4^3 =$ _____

3 marks

41. Point A is translated 3 squares right and 2 squares down. What are the coordinates of the new point A'?

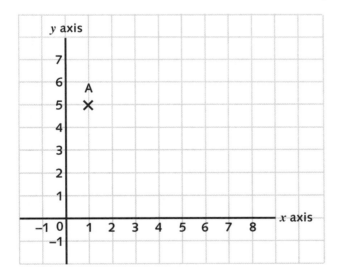

A' (_____ , _____)

1 mark

42. What is the product of 35 and 7? _____

1 mark

9

Starter Test

43. Convert the measurements.

a) 36 cm = _____ mm

b) 1060 g = _____ kg

c) 3.5 km = _____ m

d) 1.45 m = _____ cm

4 marks

PS **44.** $\frac{5}{16} + \frac{3}{16} + \frac{7}{16} = \boxed{}$

1 mark

45. Complete the equivalent fractions.

a) $\frac{3}{8} = \frac{\boxed{}}{24}$

b) $\frac{\boxed{}}{15} = \frac{3}{5}$

c) $\frac{8}{\boxed{}} = \frac{2}{3}$

3 marks

46. What is the perimeter of the tennis court?

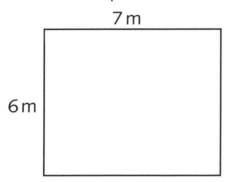

7 m

6 m

_____ m

1 mark

47. Fill in the blanks in this sequence.

| 25 | 13.5 | _____ | _____ |

1 mark

PS **48.** Phil books an 8-hour pony trek.

Pony Trekking
£8.75 per hour

How much does he pay? £_____

1 mark

10

PS **49.** Davina is buying a new carpet for her bedroom. What area of floor does she need to cover?

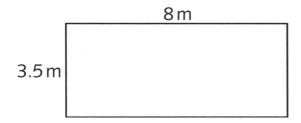

8 m

3.5 m

_____ m²

1 mark

50. What is the volume of this cuboid?

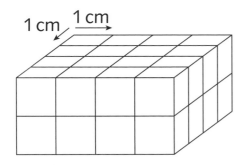

1 cm   1 cm

_____ cm³

1 mark

51. Calculate angle x.

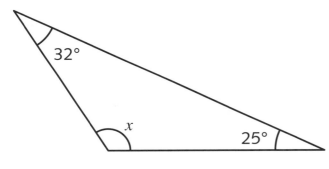

32°

x

25°

$x =$ _____ °

1 mark

PS **52.** At lunchtime my thermometer reads 6°C. By bedtime it reads −8°C.

By how many degrees has the temperature dropped? _____ °C

1 mark

53. Write $1\frac{4}{5}$ as an improper fraction.

1 mark

Marks........ /70

Place Value

PS Problem-solving questions

Challenge 1

1 Write these numbers in order from the smallest to the largest.

252	525	25	5525	2552

smallest | | | | | **largest**

1 mark

PS **2** What are the missing numbers in this sequence?

679	779		979	

2 marks

3 Write the following number in figures.

seventy five thousand six hundred and two

____

1 mark

Marks........./4

Challenge 2

1 Draw **two more** lines to match **32 000** to numbers with the same value.

32 000 → 32 000 units

320 tens
32 000 units
3200 tens
320 hundreds
3 thousands

2 marks

2 Use > and < to make these statements correct.

a) 126.2 ☐ 162.2 **b)** 166 434 ☐ 163 343

c) 5.564 ☐ 5.654 **d)** 257 979 ☐ 259 779

4 marks

Place Value

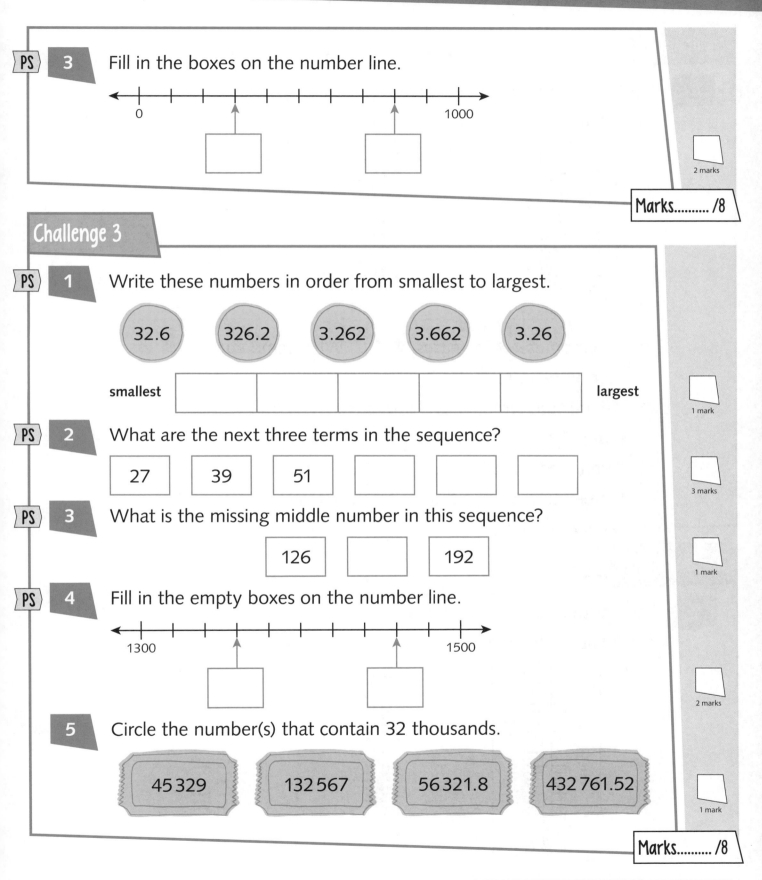

PS **3** Fill in the boxes on the number line.

0   1000

2 marks

Marks.......... /8

Challenge 3

PS **1** Write these numbers in order from smallest to largest.

32.6   326.2   3.262   3.662   3.26

smallest   largest

1 mark

PS **2** What are the next three terms in the sequence?

27   39   51

3 marks

PS **3** What is the missing middle number in this sequence?

126   192

1 mark

PS **4** Fill in the empty boxes on the number line.

1300   1500

2 marks

5 Circle the number(s) that contain 32 thousands.

45 329   132 567   56 321.8   432 761.52

1 mark

Marks.......... /8

Total marks .... /20   How am I doing?

13

Negative Numbers

Challenge 1

PS **1** Look at the thermometers below.

a) What are the readings on these thermometers?

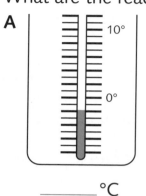 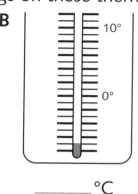 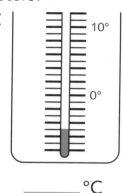

_____°C   _____°C   _____°C

b) Thermometer **A** increases by 5°C. What temperature will the thermometer read now? _____°C

c) What is the temperature difference between thermometers **B** and **C**? _____°C

d) During the night thermometer **B** drops by 10°C. What temperature will the thermometer read now? _____°C

6 marks

Marks.......... /6

Challenge 2

1 Look at the thermometers below.

a) What are the readings on these thermometers?

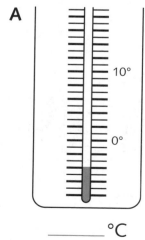 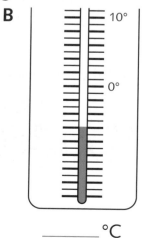 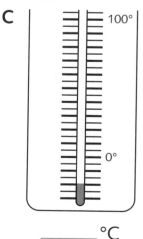

_____°C   _____°C   _____°C

14

Negative Numbers

b) Between which two thermometers is the biggest temperature difference?

Thermometers _____ and _____

4 marks

Marks.........../4

Challenge 3

PS **1** This sequence is made by **subtracting the same amount** each time. What are the three missing numbers in the sequence?

| 13 | | | | –19 |

3 marks

2 Look at this thermometer.

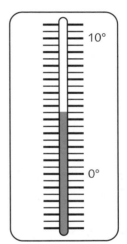

a) What is the temperature shown on

the thermometer? _____ °C

b) The temperature decreases by 8°C. Mark the new temperature on the thermometer.

c) What is the new temperature? _____ °C

3 marks

PS **3** The temperature difference between **A** and **B** is 35°C. What is the temperature at **A** and **B**?

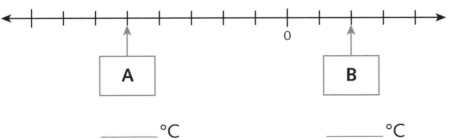

_____ °C   _____ °C

2 marks

Marks.........../8

Total marks .... /18   How am I doing?

Rounding

PS Problem-solving questions

Challenge 1

1 Round these numbers to the nearest hundred. The first one has been done for you.

376	400
2458	
3712	
2501	
2555	

4 marks

2 Circle all the numbers that would give 50 when rounded to the nearest 10.

| 51 | 42 | 45 | 48 | 59 | 55 |

1 mark

3 Round 27 163 to the nearest:

a) 100 _____   b) 1000 _____   c) 10 000 _____

3 marks

4 Circle the number that is nearest to 1000.

1935   901   1999   905   100   950

1 mark

5 What is 8 + 9, rounded to the nearest 10? _____

1 mark

Marks......... /10

Challenge 2

1 Round these decimals to the nearest whole number. The first one has been done for you.

4.20	4
5.05	
1.78	
3.19	
3.65	

4 marks

Rounding

2 What is 2211 + 435 rounded to the nearest 1000? _____

3 Round 561 728 to the nearest thousand. _____

PS **4** I think of an odd number between 20 and 26. I multiply it by 10 and round it to the nearest 100. My answer is 300.

What was my original number? _____

Marks.........../7

Challenge 3

PS **1** I need to multiply 48 x 33. Circle the rounded calculation that will best help me solve my problem.

| 50 x 40 | 40 x 30 | 50 x 30 | 45 x 35 |

2 Round 816 539 to the nearest ten thousand. _____

3 These numbers have been rounded to the nearest one decimal place. Draw lines to match them to their correct rounded equivalent. One has been done for you

2.09	4.6
3.68	3.7
4.09	2.1
3.55	3.6
4.59	4.1

4 Circle the number that is nearest to 0.09.

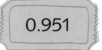 0.951   0.099   0.95   0.010

Marks.........../7

Total marks ..../24   How am I doing?

Number Problems

Challenge 1

1 What are the number bonds to 50 for these numbers?

a) 28 ☐   b) 34 ☐   c) 22 ☐

3 marks

2 Answer these.

a) 65 + 19 = ☐

b) 33 – 9 = ☐

c) 79 + 7 = ☐

3 marks

3 Find the missing numbers.

a) 75 + ☐ = 125   b) 100 – 19 = ☐

c) 175 – ☐ = 90   d) 75 – 19 = ☐

4 marks

Marks......... /10

Challenge 2

1 What are the number bonds to 1000 for these numbers?

a) 328 ☐   b) 174 ☐   c) 17 ☐

3 marks

2 Answer these.

a) 1299 + 53 = ☐

b) 101 – 75 = ☐

c) 1502 – 61 = ☐

3 marks

Number Problems

3 Find the missing numbers.

a) 57 + [ ] = 120

b) 450 – 139 = [ ]

c) 235 – [ ] = 190

3 marks

PS **4** I celebrated my 21st birthday in 2003. In which year was I born?

_____

1 mark

Marks......... /10

Challenge 3

1 What are the number bonds to 1000 for these numbers?

a) 325 [ ]   b) 811 [ ]   c) 493 [ ]

3 marks

2 a) 2465 + 59 = [ ]

b) 5199 – 175 = [ ]

c) 1999 + 78 = [ ]

3 marks

3 Find the missing numbers.

a) 203 + [ ] = 1417

b) 2211 – 139 = [ ]

c) 5239 – [ ] = 121

3 marks

Marks.......... /9

Total marks .... /29   How am I doing?   😊   😐   😣

Mental Calculations

PS Problem-solving questions

Challenge 1

1 Work out the answers to these mental calculations.

a) 50 + 30 = _____   b) 130 – 90 = _____

2 marks

2 Work out the answers to these mental calculations.

a) 199 – 50 = _____   b) 199 + 30 = _____

2 marks

PS **3** Nina has £1.99 and then finds another 65p in her pocket.

How much money does she have altogether? £_____

1 mark

PS **4** Lena spends 19p on sweets.

How much change does she get from £1? _____p

1 mark

PS **5** I have 345 football cards. I give 120 to my little brother.

How many do I have left? _____ football cards

1 mark

Marks.........../7

Challenge 2

1 a) 2100 – 50 + 180 = _____   b) 3600 + 850 = _____

2 marks

PS **2** Mike spends £2.36p on fruit. How much change does he

get from £5? £_____

1 mark

3 a) 8334 – 1300 = _____   b) 1600 + 145 = _____

2 marks

Mental Calculations

PS | **4**

Jo buys some groceries for her grandma.

£1.99　　　　　65p　　　　　£2.05

a) How much does she spend altogether? £_____

b) How much change does she get from £10? £_____

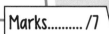
2 marks

Marks.........../7

Challenge 3

PS | **1**

Asif buys some new supplies for school.

68p　　　　　37p　　　　　91p

a) How much has he spent altogether? £_____

b) If he pays with a £5 note, how much change does he get?

£_____

2 marks

2 a) $230 - 60 + 180 =$ _____   b) $550 - 60 + 170 =$ _____

2 marks

3 a) $4600 - 750 =$ _____   b) $9345 - 99 =$ _____

2 marks

PS | **4**

Marcus had his 19th birthday on 1st January 2014. In which year was Marcus born? _____

1 mark

PS | **5**

Dougie has 299 stamps. He gives his brother 61 stamps and his sister 89 stamps. How many stamps does Dougie have left in his collection?

_____ stamps

1 mark

Marks.........../8

Total marks ..../22 　　　How am I doing?

Written Addition and Subtraction

PS Problem-solving questions

Challenge 1

PS **1**   Emily's granny visits the toy shop to buy some presents.

£12.75   £3.20   £5.45

a) How much more expensive

is a dinosaur toy than a book? £_____

b) How much does she spend

if she buys two cars and a book? £_____

c) How much does she spend

if she buys all three items? £_____

d) If she had £43.98 in her purse, how much money does she

have left after buying all three items? £_____

4 marks

Marks.......... /4

Challenge 2

1   Each box holds the total of the two boxes below it.
Fill in the blank squares.

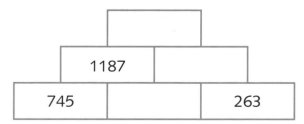

| | 1187 | |
| 745 | | 263 |

3 marks

Written Addition and Subtraction

PS **2**

Tomato sauce   £2.56
Pizza base   £1.18
Pepperoni   £3.68

a) How much does my shopping cost? £_____

b) If I had £15.67 in my purse, how much money

do I have left over? £_____

3 **a)** 785 + _____ = 1365   **b)** _____ − 213 = 1467

 2 marks

2 marks

Marks.........../7

Challenge 3

PS **1**   Brian buys some supplies for sports day.

   100 cups   100 medals   

£1.23   98p   £3.59   £4.50   £24.95

a) How much are the drinks and cups? £_____

b) How much do the prizes cost? £_____

c) Brian buys everything. How much does he spend? £_____

d) Brian has forgotten his wallet. He finds £12.48 in
his pocket. How much more money does he need

to buy all the supplies for sports day? £_____

 4 marks

Marks........../4

Total marks .... /15   How am I doing?

Addition and Subtraction Practice

 PS Problem-solving questions

Challenge 1

1 Work out the answers to these addition problems.

a)
```
   3 1 6
 + 5 4 3
 _____
```

b)
```
   4 2 7
 + 6 3 2
 _____
```

c)
```
   8 4 3
 + 1 7 1
 _____
```

3 marks

2 Work out the answers to these subtraction problems.

a)
```
   9 2 8
 − 7 1 4
 _____
```

b)
```
   7 5 7
 − 4 3 3
 _____
```

c)
```
   8 7 2
 − 5 4 1
 _____
```

3 marks

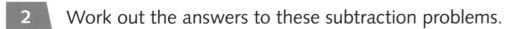

Marks.......... /6

Challenge 2

1 Now work out the answers to these addition problems.

a)
```
   3 1 7
 + 5 4 5
 _____
```

b)
```
   8 5 3
 + 9 7 8
 _____
```

c)
```
   3 9.4
 + 6 5.8
 _____
```

3 marks

Addition and Subtraction Practice

2   Now work out the answers to these subtraction problems.

a)
```
    9 2 8
  – 4 5 3
  _____
```

b)
```
    3 4 2
  – 1 5 3
  _____
```

c)
```
    8 6.4
  – 2 7.6
  _____
```

3 marks

Marks.......... /6

Challenge 3

1   Work out the answers to these addition problems.

a)
```
    1 2 5 9
  + 3 4 7 2
  _____
```

b)
```
    9.0 3
  + 9.7 9
  _____
```

c)
```
    3 9.4 7
  + 6 3.8 6
  _____
```

3 marks

2   Work out the answers to these subtraction problems.

a)
```
    1 2 0 5
  –   9 5 3
  _____
```

b)
```
    6 0 0 2
  – 1 5 4 9
  _____
```

c)
```
    1 8 0.4
  –   2 7.6
  _____
```

3 marks

Marks.......... /6

Total marks .... /18   How am I doing?

Multistep Problems

Challenge 1

PS **1** Asif and Peter visited the bakery.

Cupcakes

£6.45 per box

Biscuits

£3.68 per box

Carrot cake

£7.46 per cake

a) Asif bought a box of cupcakes and a box of biscuits. How much did he spend? £_____

b) He had £15.59 in his pocket. How much money did he have left? £_____

c) Peter bought a carrot cake and a box of biscuits. How much did he spend? £_____

d) How much more than Asif did he spend? £_____

e) What was Peter's change from £20? £_____

5 marks

Marks.......... /5

Challenge 2

PS **1** Fiona and Bella are shopping for shoes.

Trainers

£45.45

Cowboy boots

£78.99

Wellies

£23.57

a) Each week Fiona saved her pocket money to buy a pair of cowboy boots. After six weeks of saving she has £25.43 in her money box. How much more money does she need? £_____

b) Her mum gave her £55.78. How much money does Fiona have now? £_____

Multistep Problems

c) Bella bought new trainers and wellies.

How much did she spend? £_____

d) How much more did Fiona spend than Bella? £_____

e) If I bought all three pairs of shoes,

how much money would I need? £_____

5 marks

Marks.......... /5

Challenge 3

PS **1** The Smith family want to hire a boat on holiday.

Speedboat
£145.99

Canoe
£24.50

Yacht
£224.50

Rowing boat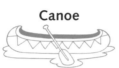
£44.25

a) If they hire the rowing boat and canoe,

how much will it cost? £_____

b) I spend £190.24 on boat hire. Which boats did I hire?

_____   _____

c) How much more does it cost to hire

the yacht than the speedboat? £_____

3 marks

PS **2** Neil's family hire the speedboat and the canoe, and Graham's family hire the yacht and the rowing boat.

a) How much did each family spend?

Neil's family: £_____   Graham's family: £_____

b) How much more does Graham's family

spend than Neil's? £_____

2 marks

Marks.......... /5

Total marks .... /15   How am I doing?

Progress Test 1

 1. In January the average night temperature is –5°C and the average day temperature is 8°C. What is the temperature difference?

_____°C

1 mark

2. Write this number in figures.

> six million, four hundred and twenty three thousand, five hundred and six

_____

1 mark

 3. Gina saves £34.56. She spends £12.24 on her friend's birthday present. How much money does she have left? £_____

1 mark

4. Brian was born in 1991. How old was he in 2012? _____

1 mark

5. What is 100 less than 1010? _____

1 mark

6. Bailey buys some new football gear. He buys a whistle, a football and some football boots.

£7.25   £8.99   £12.48

a) How much does he spend altogether? £_____

b) What is his change from £50? £_____

2 marks

7. The numbers in this sequence increase by the same amount each time. Write the missing numbers.

| _____ | 130 | 180 | 230 | _____ |

1 mark

8. 1999 + 30 = _____

1 mark

9. Circle the numbers with 25 tens.

(2531)   (3251)   (3525)   (257)

1 mark

28

10.   479
      + 896
      _____

1 mark

11. What value does the digit 2 have in these three numbers?

   a) 32456 _____

   b) 3657.2 _____

3 marks

   c) 245767 _____

12. 12200 − 250 = _____

1 mark

13. Jill subtracts 175 each time. What are the next three terms in her sequence?

   250   75   _____   _____   _____

3 marks

14. Each box holds the difference between the two boxes above it. Fill in the blanks.

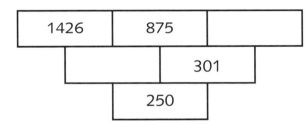

2 marks

15. Fill in the missing numbers.

   70 − _____ = _____ + 20

2 marks

PS **16.** Chloe buys some fruit.

   58p   **63p**   **47p**   **71p**

   a) How much has Chloe spent having

   bought one of each fruit? £_____

   b) How much change does she get from £5? £_____

   c) How much more expensive are oranges than bananas? _____p

3 marks

Progress Test I

17. What are the next three terms in this sequence?

14   8   2   _____   _____   _____

3 marks

18. Write this number in words.

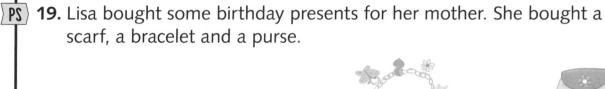

37 609

_____

1 mark

PS **19.** Lisa bought some birthday presents for her mother. She bought a scarf, a bracelet and a purse.

£24.67   £23.45   £18.99

a) How much did Lisa spend altogether?

£_____

b) What was her change from £100?

£_____

c) How much more expensive is the

scarf than the purse? £_____

d) Lisa's friend, Maggie, got £7.56 change from a £50 note. Which two items did she buy?

_____   _____

4 marks

20. Order these numbers from smallest to largest.

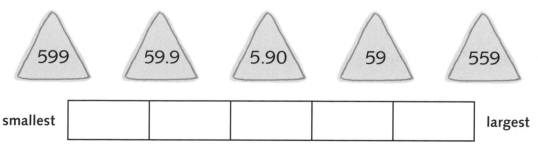

599   59.9   5.90   59   559

smallest | | | | | | largest

1 mark

30

21. What are the next three numbers in this sequence?

| 125 | 175 | 225 | ____ | ____ | ____ |

3 marks

22. 999 + 301 = _____

1 mark

23. What are the number bonds to 100?

a) 48 _____   **b)** 72 _____   **c)** 24 _____

3 marks

24. Fill in the gaps on the number line.

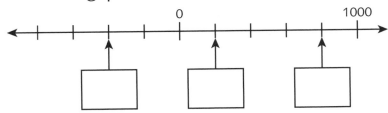

3 marks

25.
```
  18.36
-  8.52
_____
```

1 mark

26. Round 46 237.9 to the nearest:

a) ten _____   **b)** whole number _____   **c)** thousand _____

d) hundred _____   **e)** ten thousand _____

5 marks

27.
```
  2365
+ 1857
_____
```

1 mark

PS **28.** Pete's new jacket cost £47.55. Lynn's cost £63.75. How much more expensive was Lynn's jacket than Pete's? £_____

1 mark

29. What is 13 degrees lower than 6°C? _____°C

1 mark

30. Circle the answer closest to 32 + 89.

 150   200   120   220

1 mark

Marks.........../54

Factors and Multiples

Challenge 1

1 Put these numbers into the correct place in the Venn diagram.

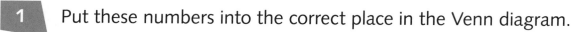

| 12 | 17 | 20 | 15 | 35 | 42 | 60 |

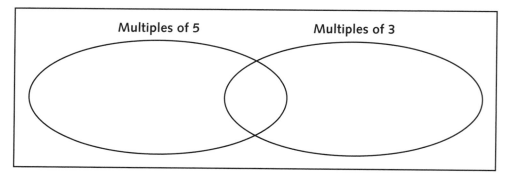

Multiples of 5   Multiples of 3

2 marks

PS **2** Circle the numbers which are factors of 18.

3   5   7   8   6   4   9

2 marks

3 Write two division facts and two multiplication facts using only these three numbers.

7   42   6

_____   _____

_____   _____

2 marks

4 Find a common multiple of both 5 and 7. _____

1 mark

Marks.......... /7

Challenge 2

1 Complete the Venn diagram by placing numbers inside the circles.

32

Factors and Multiples

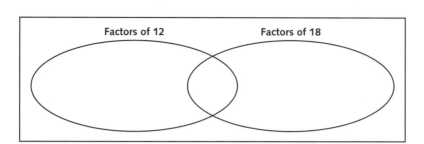

Factors of 12	Factors of 18

2 What are the common factors of 24 and 32?

_____   _____   _____   _____

2 marks

3 Find the lowest common multiple of 2, 5 and 7. _____

1 mark

PS **4** I think of an odd number greater than 5. It's a factor of both 18 and 36. What is my number? _____

1 mark

Marks.......... /6

Challenge 3

1 Here is part of a multiplication grid. Fill in the missing numbers in the empty boxes.

×	5		9
4		32	
6		48	
	60		

4 marks

PS **2** Violet's number is a factor of 27 and a multiple of 3. What is her number? _____

1 mark

3 What are the common factors of 21 and 63?

_____   _____   _____   _____

1 mark

4 What is the lowest common multiple of 3, 6 and 14? _____

1 mark

Marks.......... /7

Total marks .... /20   How am I doing?

Prime, Square and Cube Numbers

Challenge 1

1 Work out the answers to these square numbers.

a) $7^2 =$ _____ b) $6^2 =$ _____ c) $5^2 =$ _____

3 marks

2 Work out the answers to these cube numbers.

a) $2^3 =$ _____ b) $3^3 =$ _____ c) $4^3 =$ _____

3 marks

3 Peter says that 26 is a prime number. Why is Peter wrong?

_____

1 mark

4 Use >, < or = to make these statements correct.

a) 4^2 ☐ 2^2 b) 8^2 ☐ 4^3 c) 3^3 ☐ 5^2

3 marks

Marks......... /10

Challenge 2

1 Answer these.

a) $2^3 + 5^2 =$ _____

b) $4^2 + 2^3 =$ _____

c) $7^2 - 2^3 =$ _____

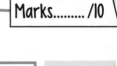

3 marks

2 Circle all the square numbers.

132   96   144   45   169   36   25

1 mark

3 Use >, < or = to make these statements correct.

a) 5^3 ☐ 9^2

b) 3^3 ☐ 6^2

c) 7^2 ☐ 4^3

3 marks

Marks......... /7

Prime, Square and Cube Numbers

Challenge 3

1 Work out the answers to these problems.

a) $3^2 + 4^3 - 5^2 =$ _____

b) $4^3 - 8^2 + 7^2 =$ _____

2 marks

2 Put a number less than 30 in each box to make the statement correct.

Prime number		Square number		Square number
☐	+	☐	=	☐

2 marks

3 Put numbers 1–20 into the Venn diagram.

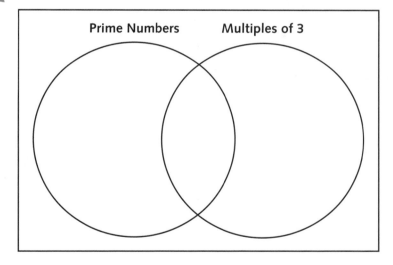

Prime Numbers   Multiples of 3

3 marks

4 Circle the prime numbers.

63   47   36   57   79   85   43

1 mark

Marks.......... /8

Total marks .... /25   How am I doing?

35

Multiplying and Dividing

PS Problem-solving questions

Challenge 1

 1 Work out the answer. 4 × (3 + 5) = _____

1 mark

2 Work out the answer to these calculations.

a) 245 ÷ 10 = _____   b) 51 × 10 = _____

c) 156 ÷ 100 = _____   d) 16 × 100 = _____

4 marks

3 Fill in the missing numbers.

a) _____ × 100 = 560   b) 1356 ÷ 100 = _____

c) _____ ÷ 10 = 34   d) 9.8 × 10 = _____

4 marks

4 Answer these calculations.

a) 810 ÷ 9 = _____   b) 50 × 30 = _____

c) 180 ÷ 3 = _____   d) 30 × 10 = _____

4 marks

5 Olivia buys four chocolate bars that cost 15p each.

How much does she pay altogether? _____p

1 mark

Marks......... /14

Challenge 2

1 Work out the answer. 6 × (9 – 3) + 8 = _____

1 mark

2 Work out the answer to these calculations.

a) 5.43 × 100 = _____   b) 6.2 × 10 = _____

c) 941.8 ÷ 100 = _____   d) 246 ÷ 10 = _____

4 marks

3 Fill in the missing numbers.

a) _____ ÷ 1000 = 7.291   b) 100 × _____ = 354

c) _____ × 10 = 47.8   d) 569 ÷ 100 = _____

4 marks

Multiplying and Dividing

4 Answer these calculations.

a) 32 × 20 = _____

b) 3600 ÷ 6 = _____

c) 300 ÷ 5 = _____

d) 60 × 30 = _____

4 marks

PS **5** Mina is putting 14 paintbrushes on each table.
If she has 168 paintbrushes, how many

tables can she supply? _____ tables

1 mark

Marks......... /14

Challenge 3

1 Work out the answer to these calculations.

a) 12 × (6 − 4) + 2³ = _____

b) 3 + (7 − 4) × 6 = _____

2 marks

2 Answer these calculations.

a) 6.754 × 100 = _____

b) 345.9 ÷ 100 = _____

c) 241.5 ÷ 1000 = _____

d) 1.3 × 1000 = _____

4 marks

PS **3** Esther has £45 to spend. If bracelets cost £4.15 each,

how many can she buy? _____ bracelets

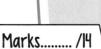

1 mark

PS **4** Luke gets paid £3.20 to wash a car.
How much will he earn if he washes 12 cars? £_____

1 mark

5 Fill in the missing numbers.

_____ × 340 = 10 × _____

2 marks

Marks......... /10

Total marks .... /38

How am I doing?

37

Written Multiplication

Challenge 1

1 What is 23 × 35? Use the multiplication grid to help you.

×	20	3
30		
5		

Total = _____

1 mark

2 Here is part of a multiplication grid. Fill in the empty boxes and calculate the total.

×	30	
50		150
	60	

Total = _____

5 marks

PS **3** To celebrate his birthday, Edward buys all his 31 classmates a cupcake. Each cupcake costs 36p.

How much does Edward spend? £_____

1 mark

4
```
    1  4  3
  ×       5
  _____

  _____
```

1 mark

Marks.......... /8

Challenge 2

1 Here is part of a multiplication grid. Fill in the empty boxes and calculate the total.

×	400		3
	12 000		
6		420	

Total = _____

7 marks

Written Multiplication

2

a)
```
    3 7
×   2 4
_____

_____
```

b)
```
    8 . 5
×       7
_____

_____
```

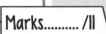
2 marks

3 Iain needs some art supplies.

Pencils

£7.32 per pack

Craft paper

43p per sheet

a) How much do three packs of pencils cost? £ _____

b) How much has he spent if he buys

45 sheets of craft paper? £ _____

2 marks

Marks.......... /11

Challenge 3

1 Fill in the blank spaces on this calculation.

```
      4 5
×     2 3
_____
  1 □ 5
□ 0 □
_____
□ □ □ □
```

7 marks

2 25 adults and 12 children go to the puppet show. How much do they pay altogether? £ _____

Puppet show	
Adults 75p	Children 35p

1 mark

Marks.......... /8

Total marks .... /27   How am I doing?

Written Short and Long Division

Challenge 1

1
a) $6\overline{)126}$ b) $9\overline{)144}$ c) $4\overline{)32.8}$

3 marks

2 Akela needs to organise 330 scouts into 15 groups for camp.
How many scouts are in each group? _____ scouts

1 mark

PS **3** Skylar, Jessie and Walter share 147 marbles between them. How many marbles do they get each? _____ marbles

1 mark

PS **4** Mr Fixit, the builder, is putting screws into boxes. If every box holds 8 screws, how many boxes will Mr Fixit need for 288 screws? _____ boxes

1 mark

PS **5** I tidy the library shelves. I put 238 books onto 17 shelves.
How many books are on each shelf? _____ books

1 mark

Marks.......... /7

Challenge 2

1
a) $16\overline{)192}$ b) $25\overline{)425}$ c) $5\overline{)71.5}$

3 marks

PS **2** Here are some prices at the supermarket.

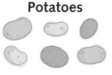

Potatoes

Tomatoes

Carrots

£6.40 per box of 8   £3.30 per box of 15   £4.16 per box of 16

a) How much is one carrot? _____p

b) How much is one tomato? _____p

c) How much is one potato? _____p

Written Short and Long Division

d) Five friends buy a box of carrots between them.

How much do they each pay? £_____

4 marks

PS **3** Jeremy spends £7.20 on party bag presents.
If a present costs 45p, how many did he buy?

_____ presents

1 mark

PS **4** Five friends hire a rowing boat for a day and
split the cost equally. How much do they

each pay? £_____

Rowing boats

£35.75 per day

1 mark

Marks.......... /9

Challenge 3

PS **1** The Roberts family need to buy some trees for their forestry
business.

Beech tree

£4.50 each

Apple tree

£7 each

Pine tree

£3.50 each

a) If they spend £76.50 on beech trees, how many

did they buy? _____ beech trees

b) If they have £98 to split equally between apple
and pine trees, how many of each can they buy?

_____ apple trees   _____ pine trees

c) New trees are delivered in lorry loads of 400.
If the Roberts family buy 9600 trees, how many

lorry loads will be delivered? _____ lorry loads

d) One lorry load of new trees costs £1312. How much

does one new tree cost? £_____

5 marks

Marks.......... /5

Total marks .... /21   How am I doing?   ☺   😐   😣

41

Multiplication and Division Practice

Challenge 1

1 Use the multiplication grids to find the answers.

a)

×	20	8
6		

$28 \times 6 =$ _____

b)

×	30	2
20		
6		

$32 \times 26 =$ _____

c)

×	40	3
20		
4		

$43 \times 24 =$ _____

3 marks

2 Work out the answers to these.

a) $7\overline{)98}$ **b)** $14\overline{)252}$ **c)** $23\overline{)552}$ **d)** $8\overline{)136}$

4 marks

Marks.........../7

Challenge 2

1 Use long multiplication to find the answers.

a)
$$\begin{array}{r} 2\ 5 \\ \times\quad 3 \\ \hline \\ \hline \end{array}$$

b)
$$\begin{array}{r} 3\ 2 \\ \times\ 2\ 4 \\ \hline \\ \hline \end{array}$$

c)
$$\begin{array}{r} 1\ 4\ 8 \\ \times\quad\ 6 \\ \hline \\ \hline \end{array}$$

d)
$$\begin{array}{r} 5\ 2\ 6 \\ \times\quad 3\ 2 \\ \hline \\ \hline \end{array}$$

4 marks

42

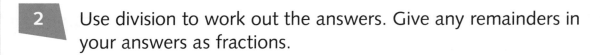

Multiplication and Division Practice

2 Use division to work out the answers. Give any remainders in your answers as fractions.

a) 6)93   b) 12)195   c) 24)648   d) 8)1088

4 marks

Marks.......... /8

Challenge 3

1 Use long multiplication to find the answers.

a)   3 7
     × 5 9
     ‾‾‾‾‾‾

b)   2 5
     × 7 . 6
     ‾‾‾‾‾‾

c)   1 4 7 8
     ×   2 6
     ‾‾‾‾‾‾‾

d)   4 5 . 2 6
     ×   2 4
     ‾‾‾‾‾‾‾

4 marks

2 Use division to work out the answers. Give any remainders in your answers as decimals.

a) 17)391   b) 24)372   c) 7)1652   d) 8)193.20

4 marks

Marks......... /8

Total marks .... /23

How am I doing?

Mixed Multiplication and Division Problems

Challenge 1

PS **1** I am buying some stationery for school.

68p   37p   91p

a) I buy three sharpeners. How much have I spent? £_____

b) I spend £1.85 on pencils. How many

   pencils did I buy? _____ pencils

c) How much will 12 rulers cost? £_____

d) If I have £6, how many sharpeners can I buy? _____ sharpeners

4 marks

2 What is £112.35 in pence? _____p

1 mark

PS **3** Seven friends share a box of 98 pumpkin seeds equally.

How many seeds does each friend get? _____ seeds

1 mark

Marks.......... /6

Challenge 2

PS **1** The teacher goes shopping for gardening supplies.

a) She buys six pairs of wellies for Year 6
   to wear in the school garden. How much
   did she spend? £_____

£14.80 per pair

b) How many pairs of gloves can I
   buy with £45? _____ pairs

£9.65 per pair

c) Year 6 buy 31 packets of seeds. How much
   do they spend? £_____

d) There are 24 seeds in each packet. How many
   seeds are there in 31 packets? _____ seeds

95p per packet

4 marks

Mixed Multiplication and Division Problems

PS **2** A bag of 15 oranges costs £4.05

How much does one orange cost? _____ p

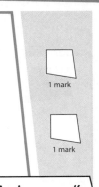
1 mark

PS **3** Apples are 57p each. How much do I pay

if I buy 12 apples? £_____

1 mark

Marks.......... /6

Challenge 3

PS **1** Here are the prices for going to the cinema.

Cinema tickets	Cost
Child	£3.55
Adult	£5.85
Student	£4.75
Family (2 adults and 2 children)	£17.50

a) Julie's mum pays for eight child tickets. How much

does she spend? £_____

b) A group of adults go to the cinema. Their tickets cost £70.20

in total. How many adults watched the film? _____ adults

c) Mike is a student at college. His tutor organises
for Mike's class of 36 students to watch a film. How much

do the tickets cost in total? £_____

d) Mr Smith, his wife and their two children want to go to
the cinema. Is it cheaper for him to buy a family ticket or
individual tickets? Explain your answer.

_____

e) Bill buys five cinema tickets. They cost £25.95 in total. What

type of tickets did he buy, and how many? _____

7 marks

Marks.......... /7

Total marks .... /19   How am I doing?

45

BODMAS

1 What does BODMAS stand for?

_____

_____

1 mark

2 Here are two identical calculations with different answers.
Put a ✓ in the box that has the correct answer.

$3 + 4 \times 2 = 14$ ☐

$3 + 4 \times 2 = 11$ ☐

1 mark

3 Work out the answers to the following calculations.

a) $2 + 3 \times 6 =$ _____   **b)** $(5 - 2) \times 7 =$ _____

c) $3 \times (2 + 6) =$ _____   **d)** $32 - 5 \times 4 =$ _____

e) $10 + 8 \div 2 =$ _____   **f)** $20 - 5 \times 3 =$ _____

6 marks

Marks.......... /8

1 Work out the answers to the following calculations.

a) $(3 + 4) \times 2 + (4 - 2) + 5 =$ _____

b) $4 + 3^2 - 5 =$ _____

c) $(7 - 3) + 4 \times 2^3 =$ _____

d) $(3 + 5) \times 8 - 8^2 =$ _____

e) $6^2 - 3 + 2 =$ _____

5 marks

BODMAS

2 Jon and James each write the same calculation but put their brackets in different places. Whose calculation gives the greatest answer? Put a ✓ in the correct box.

Jon $26 - (3 + 2) \times 4 + 3$ ☐

James $26 - 3 + 2 \times (4 + 3)$ ☐

1 mark

Marks.......... /6

Challenge 3

1 Work out the answers to these calculations.

a) $4 \times 15 - (42 - 8) + 3^2 =$ _____

b) $7 + (11 - 3) \times 4 \div 2 =$ _____

2 marks

2 Fill in the missing numbers to make these statements correct.

a) $(3 \times 8) + 12 = ($ _____ $^2 \times 10) - 4$

b) $5 +$ _____ $\times (6 \div 3) = (16 \div 4) \times 2 + 5$

c) $3^3 - 22 + 3 =$ _____ $^3 - 56$

3 marks

3 Put brackets into this calculation to make it correct.

$2^2 + 4 \times 5 + 7 \div 3 = 20$

1 mark

Marks.......... /6

Total marks .... /20

How am I doing?

Fractions

Challenge 1

1 Shade the correct amount of each fraction.

a) $\frac{1}{4}$

b) $\frac{1}{3}$

c) $\frac{3}{8}$

3 marks

2 Simplify these fractions.

a) $\frac{8}{10}$ ☐

b) $\frac{6}{24}$ ☐

c) $\frac{4}{12}$ ☐

3 marks

3 Shade $\frac{1}{4}$ of these shapes.

a)

b)

c)

3 marks

Marks.......... /9

Challenge 2

1 What fraction of the shapes is shaded?

a)  ☐

b) ☐

c) ☐

d) ☐

4 marks

2 Simplify these fractions.

a) $\frac{3}{12}$ ☐

b) $\frac{18}{24}$ ☐

c) $\frac{6}{33}$ ☐

3 marks

48

Fractions

3 Shade $\frac{3}{4}$ of these marbles.

4 Use >, < and = between these pairs of fractions to make the statements correct.

a) $\frac{3}{4}$ ☐ $\frac{6}{8}$ b) $\frac{1}{3}$ ☐ $\frac{10}{15}$ c) $\frac{5}{12}$ ☐ $\frac{4}{8}$

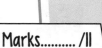

Marks.......... /11

Challenge 3

 1 The large rectangle has been divided into smaller rectangles.

a) Shade the grid as follows: $\frac{1}{4}$ black, $\frac{3}{8}$ green and $\frac{1}{6}$ blue.

b) How many rectangles of each colour are there?

Black: _____ Green: _____ Blue: _____ White: _____

2 Match the equivalent fractions. One has been done for you.

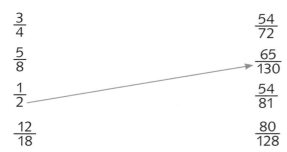

$\frac{3}{4}$ $\frac{54}{72}$

$\frac{5}{8}$ $\frac{65}{130}$

$\frac{1}{2}$ $\frac{54}{81}$

$\frac{12}{18}$ $\frac{80}{128}$

Marks.......... /8

Total marks .... /28   How am I doing?

Fractions of Amounts

 PS Problem-solving questions

Challenge 1

PS **1** Farmer Smith has 12 chickens. $\frac{1}{4}$ are black, $\frac{1}{6}$ are brown and the rest are white.

a) Shade the chickens the correct colours.

b) How many chickens are:

Black? _____ Brown? _____ White? _____

4 marks

2 Find $\frac{1}{4}$ of:

a) 16 _____   b) 12 _____   c) 20 _____

3 marks

3 Find $\frac{1}{3}$ of:

a) 9 _____   b) 24 _____   c) 60 _____

3 marks

4 Find $\frac{1}{10}$ of:

a) 20 _____   b) 100 _____   c) 90 _____

3 marks

5 Liam has 24 marbles. He gives his cousin $\frac{1}{4}$ of them.

How many marbles does he give away? _____ marbles

1 mark

Marks......... /14

Challenge 2

1 a) Shade the squares $\frac{1}{4}$ yellow, $\frac{1}{10}$ purple, $\frac{2}{5}$ green and $\frac{1}{20}$ red.

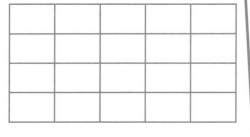

b) How many squares are:

Yellow? _____ Purple? _____

Green? _____ Red? _____

c) What fraction of the squares is not shaded?

6 marks

2 Find $\frac{3}{4}$ of:

a) 24 _____   b) 12 _____   c) 36 _____

3 marks

Fractions of Amounts

3 Find $\frac{4}{5}$ of:

a) 20 _____   b) 100 _____   c) 60 _____

4 Find $\frac{5}{8}$ of:

a) 32 _____   b) 72 _____   c) 96 _____

5 Isabelle has 105 beads. She gives her friend $\frac{2}{5}$ of them.
How many beads did she give away? _____ beads

Marks......... /16

Challenge 3

1 a) Shade the squares $\frac{1}{10}$ orange,
$\frac{1}{5}$ blue, $\frac{1}{4}$ pink, $\frac{3}{20}$ grey, $\frac{4}{25}$ green.

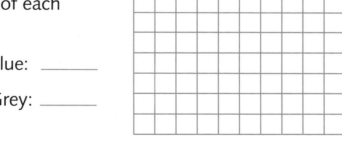

b) How many squares of each colour are there?

Orange: _____   Blue: _____

Pink: _____   Grey: _____

Green: _____

c) How many squares are not shaded? _____ squares

d) What fraction is not shaded? ☐

PS **2** Malcolm has a bag of green and blue marbles. $\frac{1}{5}$ of the marbles are green. There are 24 blue marbles.

a) What fraction of the marbles are blue? ☐

b) How many marbles are green? _____

c) How many marbles are in the bag in total? _____

Marks......... /15

Total marks .... /45   How am I doing?

Adding and Subtracting Fractions

PS Problem-solving questions

Challenge 1

PS **1** Complete these calculations. An example has been done for you.

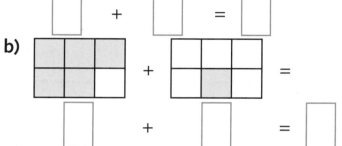

Example: ☐ + ☐ =

$\frac{1}{3}$ + $\frac{1}{3}$ = $\frac{2}{3}$

a) ☐ + ☐ =

☐ + ☐ = ☐

b) ☐ + ☐ =

☐ + ☐ = ☐

2 Work out the answers to these calculations.

a) $\frac{5}{7} + \frac{1}{7} =$ ☐   b) $\frac{4}{12} + \frac{4}{12} =$ ☐   c) $\frac{1}{5} + \frac{2}{5} =$ ☐

3 Work out the answers to these calculations.

a) $\frac{7}{15} - \frac{3}{15} =$ ☐   b) $\frac{5}{12} - \frac{4}{12} =$ ☐   c) $\frac{12}{10} - \frac{3}{10} =$ ☐

2 marks

3 marks

3 marks

Marks.......... /8

Challenge 2

1 Complete these calculations. An example has been done for you.

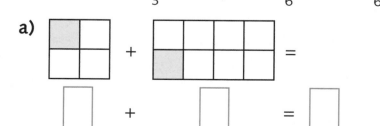

Example: ☐ + ☐ =

$\frac{1}{3}$ + $\frac{1}{6}$ = $\frac{3}{6}$

a) ☐ + ☐ =

☐ + ☐ = ☐

Adding and Subtracting Fractions

b)

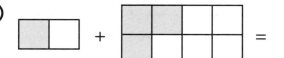 + 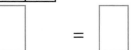 =

☐ + ☐ = ☐

2 marks

2 **a)** $\frac{2}{5} + \frac{3}{10} =$ ☐ **b)** $\frac{1}{4} + \frac{1}{2} =$ ☐ **c)** $\frac{1}{4} + \frac{3}{8} =$ ☐

3 marks

3 **a)** $\frac{7}{10} - \frac{2}{5} =$ ☐ **b)** $\frac{10}{12} - \frac{1}{6} =$ ☐ **c)** $\frac{3}{4} - \frac{1}{2} =$ ☐

3 marks

Marks.......... /8

Challenge 3

1 Complete these calculations. An example has been done for you.

Example: 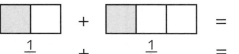 =

$\frac{1}{2}$ + $\frac{1}{3}$ = $\frac{5}{6}$

a) 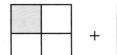 +  =

☐ + ☐ = ☐

b) 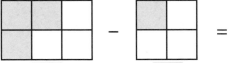 – =

☐ – ☐ = ☐

2 marks

2 **a)** $\frac{1}{6} + \frac{1}{4} =$ ☐ **b)** $\frac{3}{4} + \frac{1}{3} =$ ☐ **c)** $\frac{4}{7} + \frac{1}{3} =$ ☐

3 marks

3 **a)** $\frac{7}{15} - \frac{1}{5} =$ ☐ **b)** $\frac{9}{12} - \frac{1}{3} =$ ☐ **c)** $\frac{7}{10} - \frac{1}{4} =$ ☐

3 marks

Marks.......... /8

Total marks .... /24   How am I doing?   😊 😐 😣

Multiplying and Dividing Fractions

Challenge 1

1 Fill in the missing fractions.

a) $\frac{1}{3} \times \frac{1}{2} = \boxed{}$

b) $\frac{1}{4} \times \boxed{} = \frac{1}{8}$

c) $\boxed{} \times \frac{1}{3} = \frac{1}{12}$

d) $\frac{1}{5} \times \boxed{} = \frac{1}{20}$

4 marks

2 Fill in the missing fractions.

a) $\frac{1}{3} \times \frac{1}{5} = \boxed{}$ b) $\frac{1}{6} \times \frac{1}{3} = \boxed{}$ c) $\frac{1}{4} \times \frac{1}{2} = \boxed{}$

3 marks

3 Fill in the missing fractions.

a) $\frac{1}{2} \div 2 = \boxed{}$ b) $\frac{1}{4} \div 2 = \boxed{}$ c) $\frac{1}{3} \div 2 = \boxed{}$

3 marks

Marks......... /10

Challenge 2

1 Fill in the missing fractions.

a) $\frac{1}{3} \times \frac{1}{6} = \boxed{}$

b) $\frac{1}{4} \times \boxed{} = \frac{1}{16}$

c) $\boxed{} \times \frac{1}{3} = \frac{1}{48}$

d) $\frac{1}{5} \times \boxed{} = \frac{1}{105}$

4 marks

2 Fill in the missing fractions.

a) $\frac{1}{4} \times \frac{1}{9} = \boxed{}$ b) $\frac{1}{4} \times \frac{1}{7} = \boxed{}$ c) $\frac{1}{6} \times \frac{1}{12} = \boxed{}$

3 marks

Multiplying and Dividing Fractions

3 Fill in the missing fractions.

a) $\frac{1}{8} \div 2 = \boxed{}$ **b)** $\frac{1}{20} \div 2 = \boxed{}$ **c)** $\frac{1}{15} \div 2 = \boxed{}$

3 marks

Marks........./10

Challenge 3

1 Fill in the missing fractions.

a) $\frac{1}{12} \times \frac{1}{6} = \boxed{}$

b) $\frac{1}{4} \times \boxed{} = \frac{1}{64}$

c) $\boxed{} \times \frac{1}{3} = \frac{1}{6} \times \boxed{}$

d) $\frac{1}{5} \times \boxed{} = \frac{1}{10} \times \boxed{}$

4 marks

2 Fill in the missing fractions.

a) $\frac{1}{7} \times \frac{1}{9} = \boxed{}$ **b)** $\frac{1}{3} \times \frac{1}{15} = \boxed{}$ **c)** $\frac{1}{12} \times \frac{1}{5} = \boxed{}$

d) $\frac{1}{8} \times \frac{1}{5} = \boxed{}$ **e)** $\frac{1}{25} \times \frac{1}{4} = \boxed{}$ **f)** $\frac{1}{9} \times \frac{1}{8} = \boxed{}$

6 marks

3 Fill in the missing fractions.

a) $\frac{1}{4} \div 4 = \boxed{}$ **b)** $\frac{1}{10} \div 3 = \boxed{}$ **c)** $\frac{1}{20} \div 2 = \boxed{}$

d) $\frac{1}{20} \div 5 = \boxed{}$ **e)** $\frac{1}{48} \div 3 = \boxed{}$ **f)** $\frac{1}{64} \div 4 = \boxed{}$

6 marks

Marks........./16

Total marks ..../36   How am I doing?

Decimal Fractions

PS ⟩ Problem-solving questions

Challenge 1

PS **1** Write these fractions as decimals.

a) $\frac{1}{2}$ _____ **b)** $\frac{3}{4}$ _____ **c)** $\frac{1}{4}$ _____

3 marks

2 Write the answers to these calculations.

a) $0.035 \times 100 =$ _____ **b)** $5.8 \div 10 =$ _____

2 marks

3 What are values A, B and C?

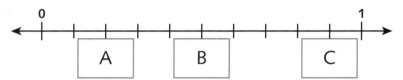

A = _____ B = _____ C = _____

3 marks

4 Round these decimals to the nearest whole number.

a) 32.8 _____ **b)** 169.4 _____ **c)** 1.43 _____

3 marks

Marks......... /11

Challenge 2

1 Write these fractions as decimals.

a) $1\frac{1}{2}$ _____

b) $\frac{1}{100}$ _____

c) $\frac{1}{8}$ _____

3 marks

2 What are values A, B and C?

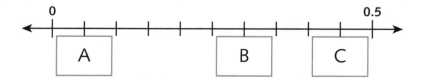

A = _____ B = _____ C = _____

3 marks

Decimal Fractions

3 Fill in the missing numbers.

a) $100 \times$ _____ $= 34.2$

b) $1050 \div 10 =$ _____

c) _____ $\times 1000 = 245.6$

3 marks

4 Round these decimals to one decimal place.

a) 38.64 _____   b) 147.26 _____   c) 2.91 _____

3 marks

Marks.........../12

Challenge 3

1 Write these fractions as decimals.

a) $\frac{35}{1000}$ _____   b) $1\frac{1}{8}$ _____   c) $\frac{1}{16}$ _____

3 marks

2 Draw labelled arrows to mark where these decimals would go on the number line.

A = 1.55   **B** = 0.05   **C** = 0.70

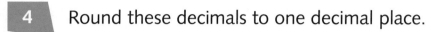

0   2

1 mark

3 Round these decimals to one decimal place.

a) 48.63 _____   b) 245.37 _____   c) 6.95 _____

3 marks

4 Fill in the boxes on the number line.

0   0.05

3 marks

Marks.........../10

Total marks ..../33   How am I doing?

Improper Fractions and Mixed Numbers

PS Problem-solving questions

Challenge 1

PS **1** $2\frac{1}{2}$ is a mixed number. Which mixed numbers do these shapes represent?

a)

b)

c)

d)

4 marks

2 $\frac{5}{4}$ is an improper fraction. Which improper fractions do the shapes above represent? The first one has been done for you.

a) $\frac{5}{4}$ b) ☐   c) ☐   d) ☐

3 marks

3 Convert these mixed numbers to improper fractions.

a) $1\frac{1}{3}$ ☐   b) $1\frac{2}{5}$ ☐   c) $1\frac{1}{2}$ ☐

3 marks

4 Circle the fractions that are greater than 1.

$\frac{1}{4}$ $\frac{7}{6}$ $\frac{3}{5}$ $\frac{10}{4}$ $\frac{1}{3}$

2 marks

Marks......... /12

Challenge 2

1 Shade the mixed numbers on the shapes below.

a) $2\frac{1}{4}$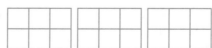

b) $2\frac{5}{6}$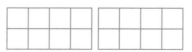

c) $1\frac{2}{3}$

d) $1\frac{5}{8}$

4 marks

58

Improper Fractions and Mixed Numbers

2 What improper fractions do the shapes in question 1 represent?

a) ☐ b) ☐ c) ☐ d) ☐

4 marks

3 Convert these improper fractions to mixed numbers.

a) $\frac{9}{6}$ ☐ b) $\frac{16}{3}$ ☐ c) $\frac{11}{4}$ ☐

3 marks

4 Give your answer to each of these problems as an improper fraction.

a) $\frac{5}{5} + \frac{4}{5} =$ ☐ b) $\frac{6}{8} + \frac{5}{8} =$ ☐ c) $\frac{3}{5} + \frac{1}{5} + \frac{2}{5} =$ ☐

3 marks

Marks......... /14

Challenge 3

1 Give your answer to these problems as a mixed number.

a) $\frac{4}{6} + \frac{7}{6} + \frac{3}{6} =$ ☐ b) $\frac{7}{8} + \frac{1}{4} =$ ☐

2 marks

2 a) $\frac{9}{5} - \frac{3}{5} =$ ☐ b) $\frac{12}{8} - \frac{1}{4} =$ ☐

2 marks

3 Put these three fractions in the correct places on the number line.

$1\frac{1}{2}$ $\frac{8}{6}$ $\frac{3}{8}$

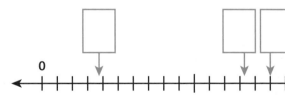

☐   ☐ ☐

0 ————————————— 2

3 marks

4 Use > and < to make these statements true.

a) $\frac{15}{12}$ ☐ $\frac{9}{6}$ b) $\frac{5}{2}$ ☐ $\frac{7}{6}$ c) $1\frac{1}{4}$ ☐ $\frac{11}{8}$

3 marks

Marks......... /10

Total marks .... /36   How am I doing? 😊 😐 😣

59

Percentages

PS Problem-solving questions

Challenge 1

1 What are the percentages represented by these fractions?

a) 1 whole _____

b) $\frac{3}{4}$ _____

c) $\frac{1}{2}$ _____

d) $\frac{1}{4}$ _____

4 marks

2 Find:

a) 25% of 32 _____

b) 50% of 64 _____

c) 75% of 40 _____

d) 25% of 160 _____

4 marks

PS **3** The sports shop is having a sale. Everything has been reduced by 25%. What are the sale prices for each item?

£60   £20   £12

a) Training top = £_____

b) Ball = £_____

c) Gloves = £_____

3 marks

Marks......... /11

Challenge 2

1 Find:

a) 10% of £135 _____

b) 30% of 180 _____

c) 80% of 80 _____

d) 40% of 120 _____

4 marks

2 Convert these fractions to percentages.

a) $\frac{8}{20}$ = _____

b) $\frac{6}{25}$ = _____

c) $\frac{8}{40}$ = _____

d) $\frac{15}{60}$ = _____

4 marks

Percentages

PS | 3 | The clothes shop is having a sale. Everything has been reduced by 30%. What are the sale prices for each item?

a) Skirt £_____

b) Trousers £_____

c) T-shirt £_____

£24 £51 £27.50

3 marks

Marks.......... /11

Challenge 3

PS | 1 | Peter got $\frac{15}{20}$ for his Maths test and $\frac{20}{25}$ for his Geography test.

In which subject did he do best? _____

2 marks

PS | 2 | Next year house prices are set to rise by 15%. What are next year's prices for these houses?

A B C

£320 000 £850 000 £648 000

You can use the tables below to help you calculate your answers.

House A			
100%	10%	5%	115%
£320 000			

House B			
100%	10%	5%	115%
£850 000			

House C			
100%	10%	5%	115%
£648 000			

_____

_____

_____

3 marks

Marks.......... /5

Total marks .... /27

How am I doing?

Mixed Fraction, Decimal and Percentage Problems

PS Problem-solving questions

Challenge 1

PS **1** I have 48 marbles. I gave my brother $\frac{1}{4}$ of them. How many

marbles did I give away? _____ marbles

1 mark

PS **2** Tom sees a T-shirt priced at £14.80 in a shop. It is reduced by 50% in the sale. What is the sale price of the T-shirt? £_____

1 mark

3 Write these fractions as decimals.

a) $\frac{8}{10}$ _____   **b)** $\frac{4}{100}$ _____   **c)** $\frac{3}{4}$ _____

3 marks

4 Shade $\frac{1}{4}$ of this shape.

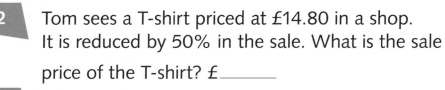

1 mark

5 Order these amounts from smallest to largest.

| £2.53 | 250p | £25 | 25p |

smallest | | | | | largest

1 mark

Marks......... /7

Challenge 2

PS **1** 400 children were asked which animal they liked best.

10% chose dogs   25% chose cats

60% chose rabbits   5% chose goldfish

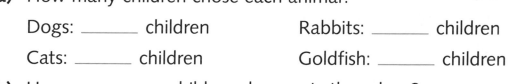

a) How many children chose each animal?

Dogs: _____ children   Rabbits: _____ children

Cats: _____ children   Goldfish: _____ children

b) How many more children chose cats than dogs?

_____ children

5 marks

Mixed Fraction, Decimal and Percentage Problems

 2 Farmer Jones has 72 cows in his herd. $\frac{5}{8}$ of his cows are brown.

a) How many cows are brown? _____ cows

b) 36 cows are white. What fraction of the cows are white? Simplify your answer.

3 Shade $\frac{3}{4}$ of this shape.

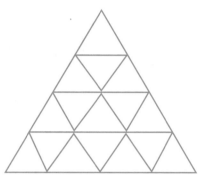

Marks.......... /8

Challenge 3

1 30% of Muhaneed's number is 18.

a) What is Muhaneed's number? _____

b) What is 65% of his number? _____

2 The value in each square is the total of the two squares below it. Fill in the blank squares.

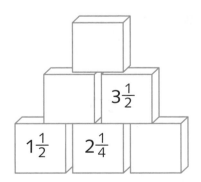

Marks.......... /5

Total marks .... /20   How am I doing?

1. Complete this calculation.

   $\frac{1}{6} \times \frac{1}{4} = \boxed{\frac{1}{24}}$ ✓

   1 mark — 1

2. Circle the prime numbers.

   32 (37) (39) 46 (53) (67) 85 (97)

   1 mark — 1

3. 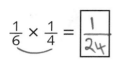 $\frac{13}{20} - \frac{3}{5} = \boxed{\frac{1}{20}}$ ✓

   1 mark — 1

4. $26.54 \times 6 = \underline{159.24}$ ✓

   $\begin{array}{r} 26.54 \\ \times \quad 6 \\ \hline 159.24 \\ 3\ 3\ 2 \end{array}$

   1 mark — 1

5. Complete the multiplication grid.

×	5	6	9
7	35	42	63
8	40	48	72
6	30	36	54

   4 marks — 4

6. Convert $2\frac{3}{5}$ into an improper fraction. $\boxed{\frac{13}{5}}$ ✓

   1 mark — 1

7. Find 80% of 150. $\boxed{120}$ ✓

   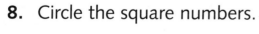
   $\times \begin{array}{r}15 \\ 8 \\ \hline 120 \end{array}$

   or $10\% = 15$
   $80\% = 8 \times 15$
   $= 120$

   1 mark — 1

8. Circle the square numbers.

   (16) 12 32 39 (25) 55 (64) ✓

   1 mark — 1

9. Write these fractions as decimals.

a) $\frac{35}{100}$ = __0.35__ ✓   b) $\frac{9}{10}$ = __0.9__ ✓   c) $\frac{20}{50}$ = __0.4__ ✓

3 marks

10. Paras is putting eggs into boxes. Each box holds 12 eggs.

How many boxes will Paras fill if he has 336 eggs? __28__ boxes ✓

1 mark

11. Convert $\frac{24}{5}$ to a mixed number. $4\frac{4}{5}$ ✓

1 mark

12. $6 + (4 \times 3) - 2 =$ | 28 | DO THE MULTIPLICATION FIRST

$6 + 12 - 2$ 16   ✗ $6 + 12 - 2 = 16$ ✓

1 mark

13. Solve 132 ÷ 5, giving your remainder as a fraction.   5)132

$= \frac{2}{5}$ ✓ $26\frac{2}{5}$ 026r2 ✓

1 mark

14. List all the factors of 36.

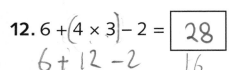 2 3 4 6 9 12 18 36 ✓

2 marks

15. Brian wants to buy a new video game costing £25 from Carl's Computers. The shop assistant notices that the box is cracked and gives him a discount of 15%. £3.75

How much does Brian pay for his game? £ __10__

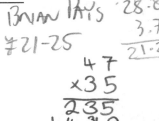
$21.25 × 15% DISCOUNT £3.75
BRIAN PAYS 28.00
£21.25   3.75
21.25

1 mark

16. 35 × 47 = __1645__ ✓

1 mark

125-16
17. $5^3 - 4^2$ = __109__ ✓

1 mark

47
×35
235
1 4 9 0
1 6 4 5

1 2 5
- 1 6
1 0 9

18. Pat buys eight bunches of flowers to decorate her restaurant.

£4.87

```
  4.87
×    8
38.96
  6 5
```

a) How much will the bunches of flowers cost altogether?

£ 38.96 ✓

b) Her business partner offers to pay half the cost.

How much do they each pay? £ 16.48 ✗ 19.48

```
 19.48
 16.48
2 38.96
```

2 marks

PS **19.** A match ticket for Pilchester Rovers FC costs £18.75
How much will I have to pay if I want to go to 25 matches?

£ 368.75 ✗ £468.75

```
 18.75
×   25
 43.75
375.00
568.75
```

1 mark

Ticket

20. $\frac{1}{9} \div 2 =$ 4 r1 ✗ 4 r1 2$\overline{)9}$ $\frac{1}{9} \div 2 = \frac{1}{9} \times \frac{1}{2} = \frac{1}{18}$

1 mark

PS **21.** George has a folder of football cards. He gives six of his friends 12
cards each. He has four cards left. How many cards were in the folder?

6 × 12 = 72 + 4 = 76 CARDS

52 cards ✗

1 mark

22. Ben records the temperature in his garden. The lowest temperature
recorded was –9°C. The highest was 7°C. What was the difference in
the two temperatures recorded?

16 °C ✓

1 mark

23. A time capsule was buried in 1899. It was dug up 105 years later.
In which year was it dug up?

2004 ✓

1 mark

24. Three children share a box of raisins. Doug has 84 raisins, Molly has 27 and Mike gets 19. How many raisins do the children have altogether?

_____130_____ raisins ✓

25. Round 42 713 to the nearest:

a) ten thousand ___40 000___ ✓

b) hundred ___42 800___ × 42 700

c) thousand ___43 000___ ✓

26. Two brothers take part in a cycling relay. Phil cycles the first 28.79 km. Brogan cycles another 57.65 km. How far do the brothers cycle in total?

_____86.44_____ km ✓   85

27. What are the next three numbers in this sequence?   + 101

700	801	902	1003	1104	1205

✓

28. Ciaran pours 1567 ml into a measuring cylinder. Max fills the cylinder up to the 2 litre mark. How much water did Max add?

_____433_____ ml ✓

30

Marks........ /37

Ratio

Challenge 1

1 What are the ratios of the hearts to clubs cards shown below?

a) _____ hearts : _____ clubs

b) _____ hearts : _____ clubs

c) _____ hearts : _____ clubs

3 marks

2 Esha puts black and white plates in a long line on the table in the ratio of **1 white : 3 black**. Shade the plates in the correct ratio.

1 mark

3 Simplify these ratios.

a) 4 : 12 _____ b) 8 : 16 _____

c) 3 : 24 _____ d) 4 : 16 _____

4 marks

Marks.......... /8

Challenge 2

1 Draw the cards in the correct ratios of hearts to clubs.

A

B

C

1 heart : 3 clubs   2 hearts : 4 clubs   4 hearts : 3 clubs

3 marks

 2 I have eight red beads and 18 blue beads. Can I make a necklace in the ratio of **2 red : 3 blue** beads and use up all my beads? Explain your answer.

_____

2 marks

PS **3** Connie visits the sweet shop.

Pear drops	Toffee
80p per 100 g	35p per 100 g

a) She buys 150 g of pear drops.

How much does she spend? £_____

b) She spends £1.05 on toffee.
How many grams has she bought?

_____ g

2 marks

Marks.......... /7

Challenge 3

PS **1** Sarah wants to send a parcel and a letter.

The parcel weighs five times more than the letter. Together they weigh 300 g. How much do the parcel and the letter weigh?

Parcel: _____ g   Letter: _____ g

2 marks

PS **2** Grace is sorting marbles into a pattern. She lines up three blue marbles followed by five green marbles.

a) If she uses 45 green marbles in total, how many blue marbles

does she use? _____ blue marbles

b) If she uses 96 marbles in total, how many of each colour has she used?

Blue: _____ Green: _____

3 marks

Marks.......... /5

Total marks .... /20   How am I doing?

Scale Factor

PS Problem-solving questions

Challenge 1

1 Peter draws a line 6.5 cm long.　　　　　　6.5 cm

He then draws another line that is 4 times longer. How long is his new line?

Length: _____ cm

1 mark

PS **2** How much longer is Sam's model than Leo's model?

Sam's model

_____ times longer

Leo's model

← 45 cm → ← 5 cm →

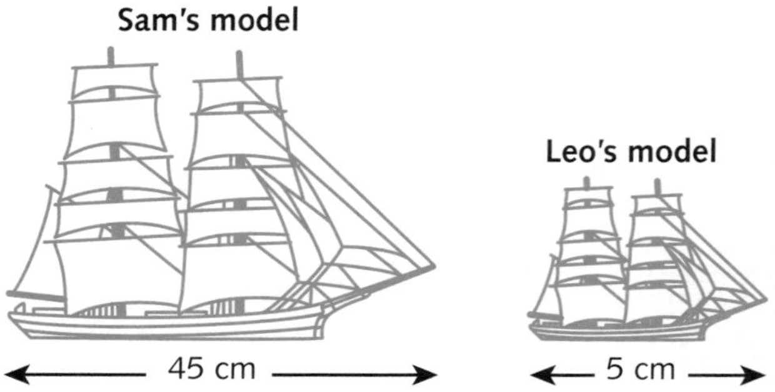

1 mark

Marks.........../2

Challenge 2

PS **1** Harvey draws a triangle eight times smaller than this one.

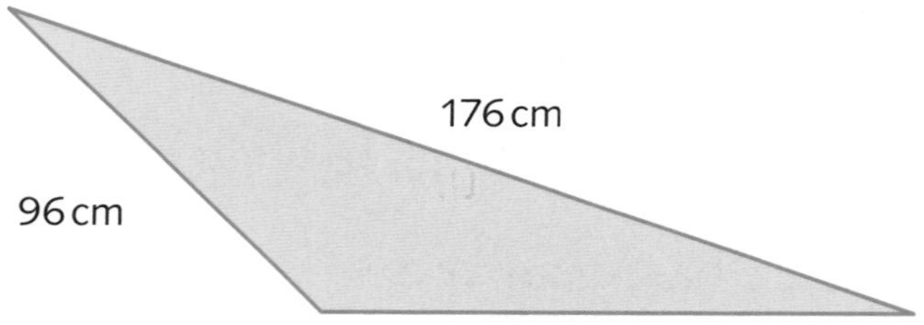

176 cm

96 cm

128 cm

What are the measurements of Harvey's triangle?

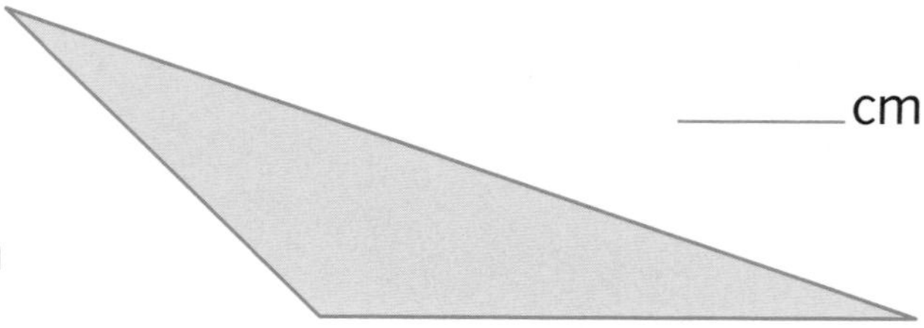

_____ cm

_____ cm

_____ cm

3 marks

Marks.........../3

70

Scale Factor

Challenge 3

PS **1** A builder is using two sizes of brick.

The big bricks measure 49 cm × 21 cm × 14 cm. The small bricks measure 7 cm × 3 cm × 2 cm. How much larger are the measurements of the big bricks than the small ones?

_____ times larger

1 mark

PS **2** Sameera is building a toy model that is 80 times smaller than the original plane. Here are the measurements of the original plane:

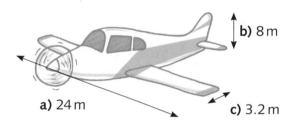

b) 8 m

a) 24 m

c) 3.2 m

What are the measurements of Sameera's model?

a) _____ m   **b)** _____ m   **c)** _____ m

3 marks

3 What are the scale factors of lines A, B and C when compared with line Z? 'A' has been done for you.

Z	A	B	C
24 cm	8 cm	264 cm	84 cm

A is _3 times smaller_ _____

B is _____

C is _____

2 marks

Marks.......... /6

Total marks .... /11   How am I doing?

Unequal Sharing

Challenge 1

PS **1** Peter is planting sunflower and bean seeds. For every one sunflower seed he plants three bean seeds. Complete the table. The first one has been done for you.

Sunflower seeds	Bean seeds
1	3
2	
5	
10	

3 marks

PS **2** This is the recipe for four servings of fruit salad. Maisie wants to make enough fruit salad for eight people. Complete the table by working out how much of each ingredient Maisie needs.

	For 4 people	For 8 people
Apples	100 g	
Grapes	120 g	
Oranges	40 g	

3 marks

Marks.......... /6

Challenge 2

PS **1** Leo is making a hotpot for dinner. The recipe gives amounts for 12 people but Leo only wants to make enough for four people. How much of each ingredient does he need?

	For 12 people	For 4 people
Beef	480 g	
Potatoes	270 g	
Carrots	150 g	
White sauce	210 ml	

4 marks

Unequal Sharing

PS **2** Farmer Adams is mixing food for his new lambs. For every three cups of grass in the mix he adds one cup of cereal. How many cups of cereal does he need to add to 27 cups of grass?

_____ cups

1 mark

Marks.......... /5

Challenge 3

PS **1** Doug has a fruity flapjack recipe for four people. If he wants to make enough for six people, how much of each ingredient does he need?

	For 4 people	For 6 people
Oats	248 g	
Butter	320 g	
Syrup	124 ml	
Sultanas	96 g	

4 marks

PS **2** James is mixing a tropical drink in the ratio of **2 mango juice : 3 orange juice : 5 sparkling water**. Work out how much of each ingredient James needs to make 1500 ml of tropical drink.

Mango juice: _____ ml

Orange juice: _____ ml

Sparkling water: _____ ml

3 marks

Marks.......... /7

Total marks .... /18   How am I doing?

Formulae and Equations

1 Work out the answers to these formulae.

a) $x + 3 = 9$ $x =$ _____

b) $y - 5 = 18$ $y =$ _____

c) $2x = 14$ $x =$ _____

3 marks

2 Work out the answers to these formulae.

a) If $x = 5$, then $4x + 2 =$ _____

b) If $x = 3$, then $3x - 4 =$ _____

2 marks

3 Complete the table. The first one has been done for you.

n	$4n - 2$
1	2
5	
10	
20	
100	

4 marks

Marks.......... /9

1 Work out the answers to these formulae.

a) $3x + 5 = 20$ $x =$ _____

b) $20 - 2y = 14$ $y =$ _____

2 marks

2 List all possible numbers for a and b.

$ab = 15$ _____

1 mark

Formulae and Equations

3 Work out the answers to these formulae.

a) If $x = 5$, solve $9x - 12$ _____

b) If $x = 9$, solve $8x + 23$ _____

2 marks

4 Work out the answers to these formulae.

$a + b = 22$ and $a - b = 6$

$a =$ _____ $b =$ _____

2 marks

Marks.......... /7

Challenge 3

1 Work out the answers to these formulae.

$5a + 76 = 111$ $a =$ _____

1 mark

2 List all possible numbers for a and b.

$ab - 12 = 20$. _____

2 marks

3 Complete the table.

n	$3n - 5$	n^2	$100n$
7			
		64	
	31		
			4500

6 marks

Marks......... /9

Total marks .... /25   How am I doing?

75

Linear Number Sequences

1 What are the next three numbers in the sequence?

 4 8 12 ___ ___ ___

2 Imogen adds the same number to her sequence each time. What is the next number in her sequence?

| 70 | 150 | 230 | ___ |

3 What is the rule for this sequence?

5   9   13   17   _____

1 What is the rule for this sequence?

11   19   27   _____

2 What are the next three terms in this sequence?

 24 15 6 ___ ___ ___

3 What are the missing numbers in this sequence?

___ 36 45 ___ 63

Linear Number Sequences

Challenge 3

1 What is the rule for this sequence?

7	11	20	36	61

2 What are the next three terms in this sequence?

23 31.5 40 ___ ___ ___

3 What are the three missing numbers in this sequence?

56 ___ ___ ___ 84

4 Look at this sequence.

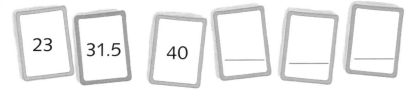

4   7   10   . . .

Term (n)	1	2	3	10	100
Number	4	7	10	___	___

a) Using the table to help you, describe the sequence in terms of n.

_____

b) What are the 10th and 100th terms of the sequence?
Write your answers in the table.

Marks.........../8

Total marks .... /15   How am I doing?

Units of Measurement

Challenge 1

1 Will's dad leaves home at this time every afternoon to get to work.

If he walks for 35 minutes, what time does he get to work? _____

☐ 1 mark

2 Convert these measures.

a) 100 cm = _____ m

b) 5500 g = _____ kg

c) 5 cm = _____ mm

d) 180 seconds = _____ minutes

☐ 4 marks

3 I pour 150 ml of squash into my jug. How much more do I need to pour in to fill it up to the 1 litre mark? _____ ml

☐ 1 mark

Marks.......... /6

Challenge 2

1 Complete the blank squares on the table.

mm	cm	m	km
		39	
45			
			1.43
	267		

☐ 6 marks

2 Ken fills his measuring jug up to the red line.

a) How many millilitres are in his jug? _____ ml

b) How many more millilitres does he need to add to fill the jug up to the 1 litre mark? _____ ml

☐ 2 marks

Units of Measurement

PS | **3** Chris completes a word search in $3\frac{1}{2}$ minutes. Oliver takes 20 seconds longer. How long did Oliver take?

_____ seconds

1 mark

Marks......... /9

Challenge 3

PS | **1** Peter runs 6.5 kilometres; his friend James runs 5 miles.

Who runs furthest? _____

1 mark

PS | **2** Hassan is $1\frac{3}{4}$ m tall and Josef is 1.6 m tall. How much taller is Hassan than Josef?

_____ cm

1 mark

PS | **3** Joe puts eight bananas on the scales below.

How much does one banana weigh? _____ g

1 mark

PS | **4** Lily's bag of dried cat food holds 1.6 kg of food. If Lily eats 40 g of food each day, how many days will the bag of food last?

_____ days

1 mark

Marks......... /4

Total marks .... /19 | How am I doing?

79

Perimeter and Area

PS **Problem-solving questions**

Challenge 1

1 Calculate the perimeter of this shape.

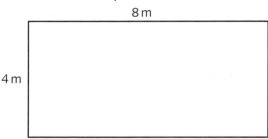

8 m

4 m

Perimeter = _____ m

 1 mark

PS **2** Amy's bedroom is 3 metres long and 2 metres wide.
Calculate the perimeter and area of Amy's room.

Perimeter = _____ m   Area = _____ m²

2 marks

3 What is the area of the school's stage?

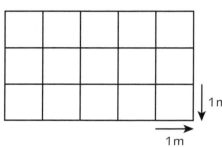

1 m

1 m

Area = _____ m²

1 mark

Marks......... /4

Challenge 2

1 Calculate the perimeter of this star.

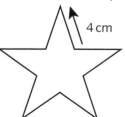

4 cm

Perimeter = _____ cm

1 mark

2 What is the area of the tennis court?

22 m

8 m

Area = _____ m²

1 mark

Perimeter and Area

3 What is the area of the shaded shape on the centimetre grid?
(1 square = 1 cm²)

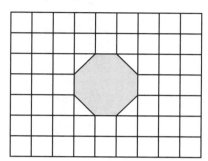

Area = _____ cm²

1 mark

Marks.......... /3

Challenge 3

PS **1** The safari park is building a
new tiger enclosure.

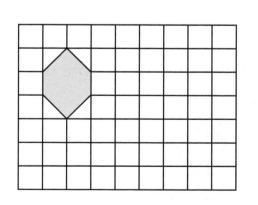

12 m

8 m

5 m

7 m

a) How much fencing do the
keepers need to buy to go
round the enclosure? _____ m

b) What is the area of the enclosure? _____ m²

2 marks

2 Draw a rectangle with the same
area as the shaded shape on
the grid.

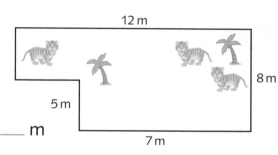

1 mark

Marks.......... /3

Total marks .... /10   How am I doing?

Area of Triangles and Parallelograms and Volume of Shapes

Challenge 1

1 Calculate the volume of this cube.

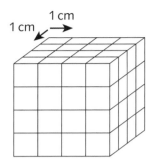

1 cm

1 cm

Volume = _____ cm³

2 What is the area of this triangle?

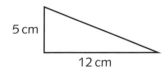

5 cm

12 cm

Area = _____ cm²

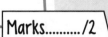
1 mark

1 mark

Marks........./2

Challenge 2

1 What is the area of this parallelogram?

8 cm

12 cm

Area = _____ cm²

1 mark

2 Calculate the area of the ship's sails.

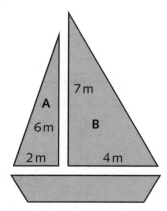

7 m

A

6 m

B

2 m

4 m

Sail **A** = _____ m²

Sail **B** = _____ m²

2 marks

Area of Triangles and Parallelograms and Volume of Shapes

3 A cube has a volume of 64 cm³. What are the lengths of its sides?

_____ cm

1 mark

Marks.......... /4

Challenge 3

1 David makes a dog out of 2-D shapes. What is the area of his 'dog'?

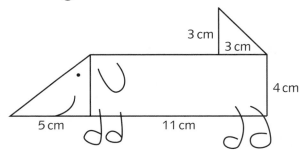

3 cm

3 cm

4 cm

5 cm   11 cm

Area = _____ cm²

1 mark

2 What is the volume of Kevin's fish tank?

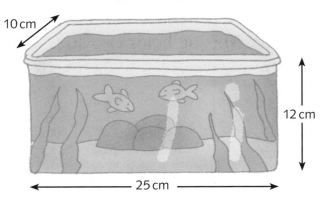

10 cm

12 cm

25 cm

Volume = _____ cm³

1 mark

Marks.......... /2

Total marks .... /8   How am I doing?

1. In each pair of measurements circle the larger one.

   a) | 200 ml | (1 pint)

   b) | 12 inches | (35 cm)

   c) | 1 km | (1 mile)

   3 marks

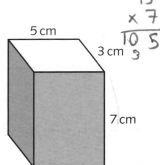

15
× 7
105

5 cm
3 cm
7 cm

PS ⟩ 2. What is the volume of Charlie's brick?

V = __105__ cm³

1 mark

PS ⟩ 3. My smoothie recipe says I need mangoes : bananas : oranges in the ratio of 2 : 1 : 3.

   a) If I use 12 mangoes, how many bananas and oranges do I need?

   __6__ bananas   __18__ oranges

   b) If I have used 78 pieces of fruit altogether, how many of each type have I used?

   __26__ mangoes   __13__ bananas   __39__ oranges

   2 marks

PS ⟩ 4. Peter is filling a jug with cupfuls of water. The jug holds two litres (2000 ml) and the cup holds 200 ml. How many cups will it take to fill the jug?

   __10__ cups

   1 mark

5. *xy* = 6. *x* and *y* are whole numbers.

   What could *x* and *y* be? __2__ and __3__

   1 mark

6. What are the next three numbers in my sequence?

7   11.5   16   <u>20.5</u>   <u>25</u>   <u>29.5</u>

PS **7.** Calculate the area of Robert's bedroom.

A = <u>27</u> m²

3 m ▭ 9 m

PS **8.** I came back from a fortnight's holiday on 5th July. On which date

did I go away? <u>21st June</u>

PS **9.** Sonia is hanging up decorations in the ratio of 3 red : 2 green : 4 white.
If she hangs up 135 decorations in total, how many of each colour does
she hang?

Red = <u>45</u>   Green = <u>30</u>   White = <u>60</u>

PS **10.** Manish starts watching TV at 4.15pm. He stops watching at 6.55pm.

For how long was he watching TV? <u>2</u> hours <u>40</u> minutes

PS **11.** Steph runs 3679 m. Jackie runs 4.53 km. How much further does Jackie

run than Steph, in metres? <u>851</u> metres

```
3 4 5 3 0
-  3 6 7 9
   0.8 5 1
```

12. What is the perimeter of this shape?

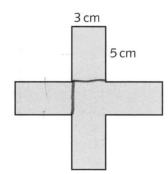

3 cm

5 cm

40
12

Perimeter = <u>52</u> cm

13. $\frac{5}{7} + \frac{2}{7} - \frac{1}{7} = \boxed{\frac{6}{7}}$

1 mark

14. Convert $\frac{8}{40}$ to a percentage. __20__ %

1 mark

15. $1600 \div 4 =$ __400__

1 mark

16. Complete the table.

3^2	4^3	3^3	9^2	5^3
9	64	27	81	125

2 marks

17. $32\overline{)1120}$ = 35

(working shown: 0035)

1 mark

18. Put these numbers in order from smallest to largest.

33.4	32.43	33.43	34.04	33.34

smallest | 32.43 | 33.34 | 33.4 | 33.43 | 34.04 | largest

1 mark

19. What are the two missing numbers in this sequence?

| −145 | −128 | −111 | | −94 | −77 |

1 mark

20. Circle the numbers that contain 23 hundreds.

8235   62 367   31 230   512 356

1 mark

PS **21.** Sui measures the temperature in her garden before she goes to bed. The thermometer reads 7°C. During the night the temperature drops by 12 degrees. What temperature does the thermometer read now?

_−5_ °C

1 mark

22. Round 615 382 to the nearest:

a) 10 _615380_

b) 1000 _615000_

c) 100 _615400_

d) 10 000 _620000_

4 marks

23. What are the number bonds to 100 for these numbers?

a) 47 _53_

b) 11 _89_

c) 86 _14_

3 marks

PS **24.** Mandy buys some items for her summer holiday.

Swimming costume

£17.99

Dinghy

£23.50

Snorkel set

£8.35

a) How much does she spend if she buys the dinghy and the snorkel set? £_31.85_

$$\begin{array}{r} 23.50 \\ 17.99 \\ +\ 8.35 \\ \hline 49.84 \end{array}$$

b) She spends £26.34. Which two items did she buy?

Swimming costume _Snorkel set_

c) How much does she spend if she buys all three items? £_49.84_

3 marks

Marks........ /37

87

2-D Shapes

Challenge 1

1 Here is part of a square. Complete the drawing by adding another two sides.

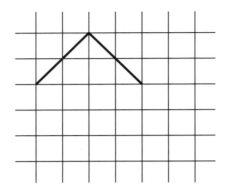

1 mark

2 Here is a triangle. Tick the **two** correct statements.

All of its angles are equal.

It has two equal sides.

Its angles all add up to 180°.

2 marks

Marks.........../3

Challenge 2

1 Calculate angle x.

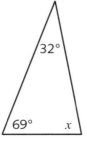

$x =$ _____ °

1 mark

2 Here is part of a parallelogram. Complete the drawing by adding another two sides.

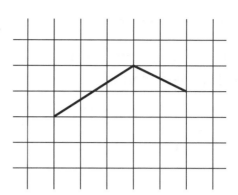

1 mark

Marks............/2

1 Here is part of a trapezium. Complete the drawing by adding another two sides.

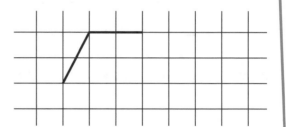

1 mark

2 Here are some 2-D shapes. Put the correct letters beside the statements below.

  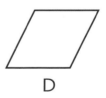

    A   B   C   D

a) Has only two sets of parallel sides _____

b) Has no right angles _____

c) Only has two acute angles and two obtuse angles _____

d) Only has obtuse angles _____

4 marks

Marks.........../5

Total marks ..../10   How am I doing?

3-D Shapes and Nets

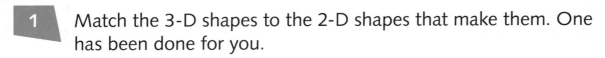

PS Problem-solving questions

Challenge 1

1 Match the 3-D shapes to the 2-D shapes that make them. One has been done for you.

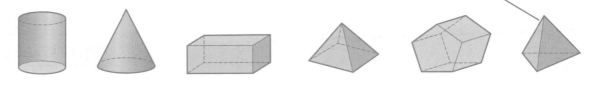

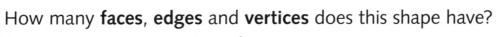

5 marks

2 How many **faces**, **edges** and **vertices** does this shape have?

Faces: _____   Edges: _____   Vertices: _____

3 marks

Marks.......... /8

Challenge 2

1 This is an incomplete net of a tetrahedron. Complete the net.

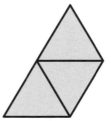

1 mark

3-D Shapes and Nets

2 This is a net of a 3-D shape. How many **faces**, **edges** and **vertices** does the 3-D shape have?

Faces: _____   Edges: _____   Vertices: _____

3 marks

PS **3** Connie thinks of a 3-D shape. She says, 'It has 6 faces, 12 edges and 8 vertices. Its faces are two different 2-D shapes.'

What is Connie's shape? _____

1 mark

Marks.......... /5

Challenge 3

PS **1** Peter has two identical tetrahedrons. He joins the two shapes by putting the bases together to make a new 3-D shape. How many faces, edges and vertices does his new shape have?

Faces: _____

Edges: _____

Vertices: _____

3 marks

2 Here is a patterned cube. Draw the missing pattern on the net below.

1 mark

Marks......... /4

Total marks .... /17   How am I doing?

Circles

PS Problem-solving questions

Challenge 1

1 What is the diameter of a circle if the radius is 4 cm?

_____ cm

4 cm

1 mark

2 What is the radius of the circle if the diameter is 12 m?

_____ m

12 m

1 mark

PS **3** Amelia lays 12 coins next to each other in a long line.

Each coin has a diameter of 2 cm.

2 cm

How long is her line of coins?

_____ cm

1 mark

Marks.........../3

Challenge 2

PS **1** What is the radius of Farmer Smith's cartwheel?

2.5 m

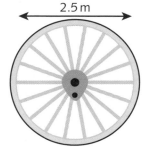

_____ m

1 mark

PS **2** Samiya's bracelet is made with beads with a diameter of 1.5 cm.
If her bracelet measures 15 cm, how many beads are on it?

_____ beads

1 mark

Circles

3 Peter lays 12 plates in a line along a table. The line of plates measures 6 m. What is the radius and diameter of each plate?

Radius = _____ cm   Diameter = _____ cm

 2 marks

Marks.......... /4

Challenge 3

 1 Kamal has a collection of different coins.

He puts the coins edge to edge to make a long line. He uses three 5p coins, seven 10p coins and four 20p coins. What does his line of coins measure?

Diameter 2 cm	Radius 0.5 cm	Radius 0.75 cm

_____ cm

1 mark

PS **2** Alana has a necklace made from 20 circular beads. It measures 38 cm in length. What is the radius of each bead?

_____ cm

1 mark

3 The circumference of a circle can be calculated by using the formula:

$$c = 3.14 \times d$$
where c = circumference and d = diameter

c = 44 cm

Which of the following measurements is the **radius** of this circle? Tick ✓ the correct answer.

12 cm [ ]   7 cm [ ]   14 cm [ ]

 1 mark

Marks......... /3

Total marks .... /10   How am I doing?

Missing Angles

Challenge 1

1 Calculate angle x.

a)

b) 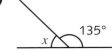 135°

c) 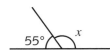 55° x

a) $x =$ _____ °   **b)** $x =$ _____ °   **c)** $x =$ _____ °

3 marks

2 Measure angle x using a protractor.

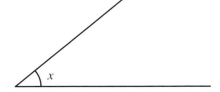

$x =$ _____ °

1 mark

3 Calculate angle x.

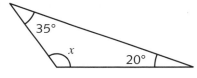
35° x 20°

$x =$ _____ °

1 mark

Marks.......... /5

Challenge 2

1 Estimate angle x. Circle the measurement that is the closest.

20°   110°   50°   85°

x

1 mark

2 Calculate angle x.

a)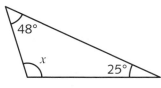
48° x 25°

Angle $x =$ _____ °

94

Missing Angles

b)

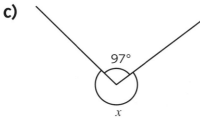

Angle $x =$ _____ °

c)

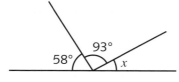

Angle $x =$ _____ °

3 marks

Marks.......... /4

Challenge 3

1 Calculate angles x and y.

a)

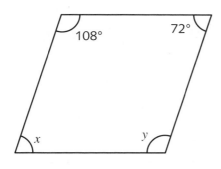

Angle $x =$ _____ °

Angle $y =$ _____ °

b)

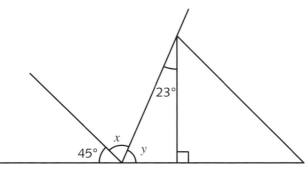

Angle $x =$ _____ °

Angle $y =$ _____ °

4 marks

Marks.......... /4

Total marks .... /13   How am I doing?

Coordinates

1 **a)** Plot these points on the grid.

A (2,1)   B (2,5)   C (5,1)   D (5,5)

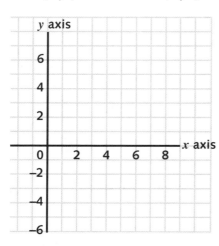

b) Join the points with straight lines. What shape is ABCD?

_____

c) What are the coordinates of the point halfway between A

and B? (_____ , _____)

6 marks

Marks.......... /6

1 **a)** Plot these points on the grid.

A (–5,1)

B (–3,5)

C (3,1)

D (1,–3)

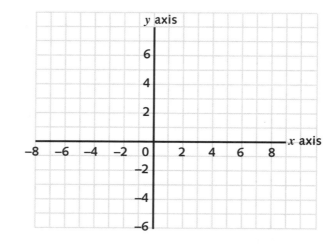

b) Join the points with straight lines. What shape is ABCD?

_____

c) Find the point halfway along line AD. What are its coordinates? (_____ , _____)

6 marks

Marks.......... /6

1 **a)** Plot these points on the grid and join them with a straight line.

A   (6,–3)   B   (–4,5)

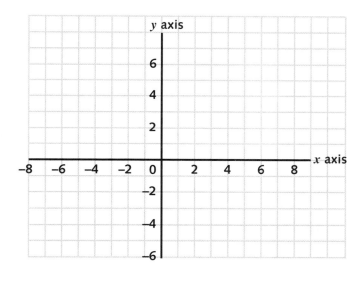

2 marks

b) Point Z is the midpoint of the line AB. Plot point Z.

c) What are the coordinates of point Z? (_____ , _____)

d) ABC is a triangle with a right angle at C. Draw triangle ABC.

e) What are the coordinates of point C? (_____ , _____)

5 marks

Marks.......... /7

Total marks .... /19   How am I doing?

Translation

1   **a)** What are the coordinates of the vertices of shape A?

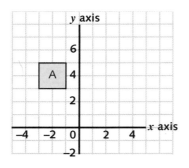

(_____ , _____)   (_____ , _____)

(_____ , _____)   (_____ , _____)

b) Translate shape A 4 squares right to become shape A′.

c) Give the coordinates of the vertices of A′.

(_____ , _____)   (_____ , _____)

(_____ , _____)   (_____ , _____)

9 marks

Marks.......... /9

1   **a)** What are the coordinates of the vertices of shape A?

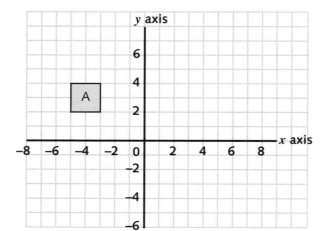

(_____ , _____)

(_____ , _____)

(_____ , _____)

(_____ , _____)

b) Translate shape A 4 squares right and 3 squares down to become shape A'.

c) Give the coordinates of A'.

(_____ , _____)   (_____ , _____)

(_____ , _____)   (_____ , _____)

9 marks

Marks.......... /9

Challenge 3

1 **a)** Give the coordinates of the vertices of shape A'.

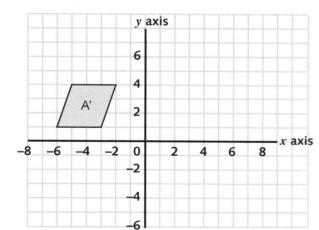

(_____ , _____)

(_____ , _____)

(_____ , _____)

(_____ , _____)

b) Shape A' is the result of the translation of shape A. Shape A was translated 8 squares left and 3 squares up, to produce shape A'. Draw shape A.

c) Give the coordinates of the vertices of shape A.

(_____ , _____)   (_____ , _____)

(_____ , _____)   (_____ , _____)

9 marks

Marks.......... /9

Total marks .... /27   How am I doing?

Reflection

Challenge 1

1 **a)** Give the coordinates of the vertices of shape A.

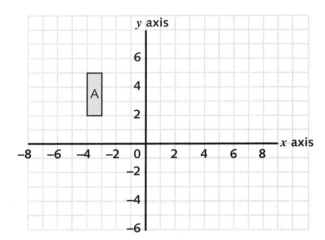

(_____ , _____)

(_____ , _____)

(_____ , _____)

(_____ , _____)

b) Reflect shape A in the *x*-axis to give shape A'. Draw shape A'.

c) Give coordinates for the vertices of shape A'.

(_____ , _____)   (_____ , _____)

(_____ , _____)   (_____ , _____)

9 marks

Marks.......... /9

Challenge 2

1 **a)** Give the coordinates of shape A.

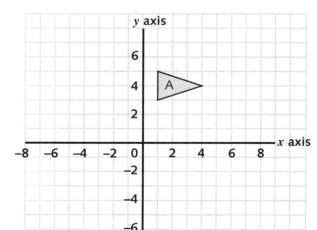

(_____ , _____)

(_____ , _____)

(_____ , _____)

Reflection

b) Reflect shape A in the y-axis to give shape A′. Draw shape A′.

c) Give coordinates of the vertices of shape A′.

(_____ , _____)   (_____ , _____)   (_____ , _____)

7 marks

Marks.......... /7

Challenge 3

1 Shape A was reflected in the x-axis to produce B.

Shape B was then reflected in the y-axis to produce shape C.

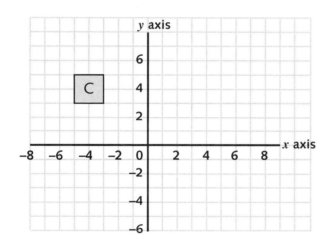

a) Plot and draw shapes A and B.

b) Give coordinates of the vertices of shapes A and B.

Shape A   Shape B

(_____ , _____)   (_____ , _____)

(_____ , _____)   (_____ , _____)

(_____ , _____)   (_____ , _____)

(_____ , _____)   (_____ , _____)

10 marks

Marks.......... /10

Total marks .... /26   How am I doing?

101

Line Graphs

Challenge 1

1 Scientists measured the temperature between 10am and 10pm.

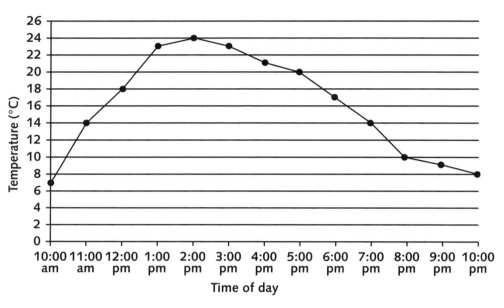

a) In what units was the temperature measured?

_____

b) At what time was the lowest temperature recorded? _____

c) What was the temperature at 12 noon? _____°C

d) At what time was the highest temperature recorded?

_____

e) How much hotter was it at 5pm than at 8pm? _____°C

5 marks

Marks.........../5

Challenge 2

1 Look at the graph in Challenge 1.

a) What was the temperature difference between 3pm and

9pm? _____°C

b) How many temperature recordings were made?

_____ recordings

c) At what times was the second highest temperature recorded?

_____

d) At what times was the same temperature recorded?

_____   _____

e) If the temperature dropped a further 8 degrees from 10pm until 2am, what would be the temperature at 2am?

_____

5 marks

Marks.......... /5

Challenge 3

1 Look at the graph in Challenge 1.

a) What was the average temperature from 10am to 1pm?

_____°C

b) On how many occasions was a temperature of more than 12°C recorded? _____

c) Estimate the temperature at 12.30pm _____°C

d) Which times had temperatures of 10°C or less recorded?

_____   _____

_____   _____

e) During the night the temperature dropped to –2°C. How many degrees did the temperature drop from 10pm? _____°C

5 marks

Marks.......... /5

Total marks .... /15   How am I doing?

Pie Charts

Challenge 1

1 60 children in Year 6 take music lessons. The information is presented in a pie chart.

Music lessons in Year 6

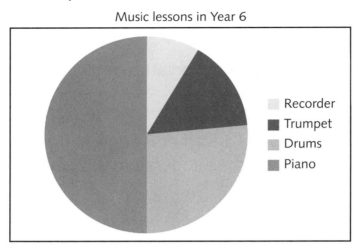

Recorder
Trumpet
Drums
Piano

a) Which is the most popular instrument? _____

b) Which is the least popular instrument? _____

c) What fraction of children play the piano? _____

d) How many children play the piano? _____ children

e) If five children play the recorder, estimate how many children play the trumpet? _____ children

5 marks

Marks.......... /5

Challenge 2

1 Look at the pie chart in Challenge 1.

a) Circle the fraction of children that play the drums.

 $\frac{1}{2}$ $\frac{3}{5}$ $\frac{1}{4}$ $\frac{4}{15}$ $\frac{2}{3}$

b) How many children play the drums? _____ children

c) How many more children play the piano than the recorder?

_____ children

3 marks

104

Pie Charts

2 Present the information below by colouring the pie chart and key.

Type of fruit	Number
Apple	3
Orange	1
Banana	2
Total	6

Key: Apple [ ]   Orange [ ]   Banana [ ]

3 marks

Marks.......... /6

Challenge 3

1 Complete the table below by calculating the percentage (%) and number of degrees for each pet.

Favourite pet	Number	%	Degrees / 360
Cat	100		
Stick insect	10		
Budgie	40		
Dog	50		
Total	200	100	360

8 marks

2 Using a protractor, present the information from the table as a pie chart and key.

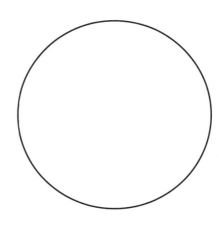

Key:

[ ] Cat   [ ] Stick insect

[ ] Budgie   [ ] Dog

4 marks

Marks........ /12

Total marks .... /23   How am I doing?

105

Calculating Mean

Challenge 1

1 Calculate the mean of these three numbers.

 7   8   3   _____

1 mark

PS **2** Ryan has 12 sweets, Neil has 11 and Connor has 7.
What is the average number of sweets that the boys have?

_____ sweets

1 mark

3 What is the mean price of the fruit?

50p   15p   25p   10p   _____p

1 mark

4 What is the average number of goals scored per game by

Badger Town FC? _____ goals

Game	1	2	3	4	5
Goals scored	5	2	4	6	3

1 mark

Marks.......... /4

Challenge 2

1 What is the mean weight of the parcels?

150 g   50 g   300 g   100 g   _____ g

1 mark

2 The mean of a set of four numbers is 14. What is the
missing number?

 13   16   17   ⭐

1 mark

Calculating Mean

3 Here is a table of some Year 6 children and their heights.

Name	Height (cm)
Zamaan	132
Sophie	144
Alex	149
Sammy	155

What is the average height of these children? _____ cm

1 mark

Marks.......... /3

Challenge 3

1 Greg is practising his long jumps. He has five attempts.

Attempt	1	2	3	4	5
Distance (cm)	350	300	395	325	330

What is his average jumping distance? _____ cm

1 mark

PS **2** Adele is working in a pottery making mugs. Here is a table showing how many mugs she made each day.

Mon	Tue	Wed	Thurs	Fri
8	11	14	13	?

If Adele wants to produce an average of 12 mugs per day,

how many must she make on Friday? _____ mugs

1 mark

3 What is the mean price of the gift boxes?

Large box

Small box

Medium box

£5.45   **£3.38**   **£4.16**   £_____

1 mark

Marks.......... /3

Total marks .... /10   How am I doing?

PS **1.** Year 6 did a survey on fast food. They asked a class of 32 students about their favourite foods.

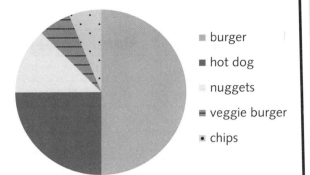

- burger
- hot dog
- nuggets
- veggie burger
- chips

    a) How many chose hot dogs?

        _____ students

    b) What fraction of the class chose chips?

    c) How many chose nuggets? _____ students

3 marks

2. What 3-D shape does this make?

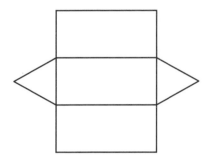

_____

1 mark

3. Find the mean of this set of data.

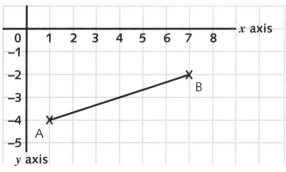

12   15   16   12   10

_____

1 mark

4. What are the coordinates of the point halfway between point A and point B?

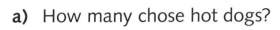

(_____ , _____)

1 mark

5. Calculate angle x.

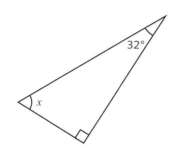

$x =$ _____

6. What is the radius of this circle?

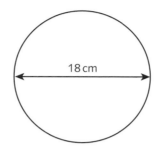

18 cm

_____ cm

7.

Miles per gallon of fuel

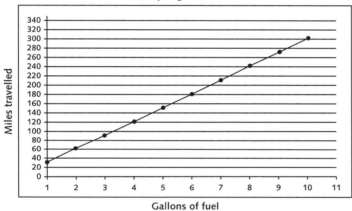

Gallons of fuel

a) How many miles could I travel on 2 gallons of fuel? _____ miles

b) If I drive 240 miles, how much fuel will my car have used?

_____ gallons

c) Estimate how far I could drive on 11 gallons of fuel. _____ miles

d) How many gallons will I use if I drive 270 miles? _____ gallons

e) Estimate how many miles I can travel on 3.5 gallons of fuel.

_____ miles

8. $\frac{3}{8} + \frac{1}{4} + \frac{5}{16} =$ ☐

9. Bill has a bag of 24 marbles. 6 are blue, 12 are red, 3 are black and 3 are green. What are the percentages of each colour?

Blue = _____%   Red = _____%

Black = _____%   Green = _____%

10. The sides of my rectangle are in the ratio 1:3.
My rectangle is scaled up by a factor of 4.
What is the **length** of my new rectangle, shown below?

3 cm

_____ cm

2 marks

1 mark

11. $4x + 12 = 36$ $x =$ _____

12. A shape is drawn on 1 cm square paper

  a) What is the area of the shaded shape?

    A = _____ cm²

  b) What is the perimeter of the shaped shape?

    P = _____ cm

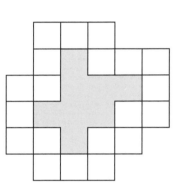

2 marks

13. My pasta recipe for 12 people is as follows. How much of each ingredient do I need to make it for only three people? Complete the table.

	12 people	3 people
Pasta	200 g	
Ham	96 g	
Cheese	120 g	
Cream	180 ml	

4 marks

14. If $5n - 8 = 27$, what does n equal?

   $n =$ _____

1 mark

15. What is the next number in the sequence?

4   5   7   10   14   ___

1 mark

16. What is the capacity of Farmer Biggs's water trough?

15 cm

30 cm

20 cm

V = _____ cm³

 1 mark

17. Shelley takes her cake out of the oven at 3.25pm. It baked for 2 hours and 20 minutes. At what time did Shelley put her cake into the oven?

_____

1 mark

18. What is 3451 + 144 rounded to the nearest 100?

_____

1 mark

19. Work out the answers to these mental calculations.

    a) 110 – 50 = _____   **b)** 299 + 147 = _____

2 marks

PS **20.** Guenna spends £5.47 on a cake tin and two biscuit cutters. The cake tin costs £3.21. How much does one biscuit cutter cost?

    £_____

1 mark

PS **21.** Peter was born in 1999. How old is Peter on his birthday in the following years?

    a) 2011 _____   **b)** 2085 _____

    c) 2036 _____

3 marks

PS **22.** These two thermometers show temperatures in °C.

    a) What are the two temperatures shown?

    _____°C

    _____°C

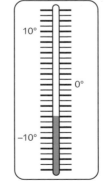 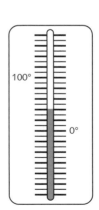

10°

0°

–10°

100°

0°

    b) What is the temperature difference between the two thermometers?

    _____°C

3 marks

Marks......... /41

111

Notes

Answers

Pages 4–11
Starter Test
1   2.44, 2.45, 2.52, 2.54, 5.25
2   £1.55
3   48
4   15 shelves
5   $\frac{29}{8}$
6   750 ml
7   2221
8   6 sides
9   159
10 A = 150, B= 400
11 93p
12 307 001
13 £3450
14 48
15 a) Terry
    b) 166
    c) 36
16 8.10am
17 $5\frac{1}{3}$
18 a) 5180
    b) 5200
    c) 5000
19 a) cube   b) cuboid
20 £3.03
21 $\frac{1}{4}$, $\frac{5}{12}$, $\frac{1}{2}$, $\frac{4}{6}$
22 £34.48
23

24 540°
25 27th Nov
26 a) 0.75
    b) 0.3
    c) 0.056
27 B and C
28 £48.60
29 95 seconds
30 £2.70
31 10
32 1, 2 ,4, 8, 16, 32
33 844 g
34 Any two numbers that total 20.
    For example: 19 and 1.
35 4 weeks
36 Any 2 squares shaded.

37 9610
38 ③, 25, ㉛, 42, 51, ㊲, 75
39 a) 3.3
    b) 100
    c) 33
40 a) 27
    b) 144
    c) 64
41 (4,3)
42 245
43 a) 360 mm
    b) 1.06 kg
    c) 3500 m
    d) 145 cm
44 $\frac{15}{16}$
45 a) $\frac{9}{24}$
    b) $\frac{9}{15}$
    c) $\frac{8}{12}$
46 26 m
47 25, 13.5, **2**, **–9.5**
48 £70
49 28 m²
50 32 cm³
51 123°
52 14°C
53 $\frac{9}{5}$

Pages 12–13
Challenge 1
1   25, 252, 525, 2552, 5525
2   679, 779, **879**, 979, **1079**
3   75 602
Challenge 2
1
    $$32\,000 \begin{cases} 320 \text{ tens} \\ 32\,000 \text{ units} \\ 3200 \text{ tens} \\ 320 \text{ hundreds} \\ 3 \text{ thousands} \end{cases}$$
2   a) 126.2 < 162.2
    b) 166 434 > 163 343
    c) 5.564 < 5.654
    d) 257 979 < 259 779
3   300, 800
Challenge 3
1   3.26, 3.262, 3.662, 32.6, 326.2
2   27, 39, 51, **63**, **75**, **87**
3   159
4   1360, 1460
5   132 567, 432 761.52

Answers

Pages 14–15
Challenge 1
1 a) –2°C, –7°C, –5°C
   b) 3°C
   c) 2°C
   d) –17°C
Challenge 2
1 a) –4°C, –6°C, –20°C
   b) A and C
Challenge 3
1 13, **5**, **–3**, **–11**, –19
2 a) 4.5°C
   b) –3.5°C marked clearly on thermometer
   c) –3.5°C
3 A = –25°C, B = 10°C

Pages 16–17
Challenge 1
1

376	400
2458	**2500**
3712	**3700**
2501	**2500**
2555	**2600**

2 (51), 42, (45), (48), 59, 55
3 a) 27 200   b) 27 000
   c) 30 000
4 950
5 20
Challenge 2
1

4.20	4
5.05	**5**
1.78	**2**
3.19	**3**
3.65	**4**

2 3000
3 562 000
4 25
Challenge 3
1 (50 × 30)
2 820 000
3 2.09   4.6
   3.68   3.7
   4.09   2.1
   3.55   3.6
   4.59   4.1
4 (0.099)

Pages 18–19
Challenge 1
1 a) 22   b) 16
   c) 28
2 a) 84   b) 24
   c) 86
3 a) 50   b) 81
   c) 85   d) 56
Challenge 2
1 a) 672   b) 826
   c) 983
2 a) 1352   b) 26
   c) 1441
3 a) 63   b) 311
   c) 45
4 1982
Challenge 3
1 a) 675   b) 189
   c) 507
2 a) 2524   b) 5024
   c) 2077
3 a) 1214   b) 2072
   c) 5118

Pages 20–21
Challenge 1
1 a) 80   b) 40
2 a) 149   b) 229
3 £2.64
4 81p
5 225
Challenge 2
1 a) 2230   b) 4450
2 £2.64
3 a) 7034   b) 1745
4 a) £4.69   b) £5.31
Challenge 3
1 a) £1.96   b) £3.04
2 a) 350   b) 660
3 a) 3850   b) 9246
4 1995
5 149 stamps

Pages 22–23
Challenge 1
1 a) £7.30   b) £11.85
   c) £21.40   d) £22.58
Challenge 2
1

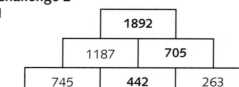

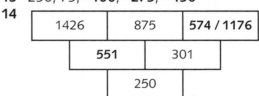

2 **a)** £7.42   **b)** £8.25
3 **a)** 580   **b)** 1680
Challenge 3
1 **a)** £5.80   **b)** £29.45
   c) £35.25   **d)** £22.77

Pages 24–25
Challenge 1
1 **a)** 859   **b)** 1059
   c) 1014
2 **a)** 214   **b)** 324
   c) 331
Challenge 2
1 **a)** 862   **b)** 1831
   c) 105.2
2 **a)** 475   **b)** 189
   c) 58.8
Challenge 3
1 **a)** 4731   **b)** 18.82
   c) 103.33
2 **a)** 252   **b)** 4453
   c) 152.8

Pages 26–27
Challenge 1
1 **a)** £10.13   **b)** £5.46
   c) £11.14   **d)** £1.01
   e) £8.86
Challenge 2
1 **a)** £53.56   **b)** £81.21
   c) £69.02   **d)** £9.97
   e) £148.01
Challenge 3
1 **a)** £68.75
   b) Speedboat and rowing boat
   c) £78.51
2 **a)** Neil's family: £170.49, Graham's family:
   £268.75
   b) £98.26

Pages 28–31
Progress Test 1
1 13°C
2 6 423 506
3 £22.32
4 21 or 20
5 910
6 **a)** £28.72
   b) £21.28
7 **80**, 130, 180, 230, **280**
8 2029
9 3251, 257
10 1375

11 **a)** thousands
   b) tenths
   c) hundred thousands
12 11 950
13 250, 75, **–100, –275, –450**
14

1426	875	**574 / 1176**

551	301

250

15 Any two numbers which have a sum of 50.
For example: 1 and 49.
16 **a)** £2.39
   b) £2.61
   c) 8p
17 14, 8, 2, **–4, –10, –16**
18 thirty seven thousand six hundred and nine
19 **a)** £67.11
   b) £32.89
   c) £5.68
   d) Bracelet and purse
20 5.90, 59, 59.9, 559, 599
21 125, 175, 225, **275, 325, 375**
22 1300
23 **a)** 52
   b) 28
   c) 76
24 –400, 200, 800
25 9.84
26 **a)** 46 240
   b) 46 238
   c) 46 000
   d) 46 200
   e) 50 000
27 4222
28 £16.20
29 –7°C
30 (120)

Pages 32–33
Challenge 1
1
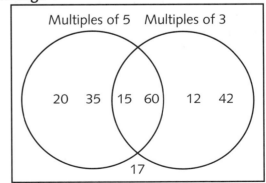

Answers

2 ③, ⑥, ⑨
3 $7 \times 6 = 42$, $6 \times 7 = 42$, $42 \div 7 = 6$, $42 \div 6 = 7$
4 35, 70, 105... and so on

Challenge 2
1
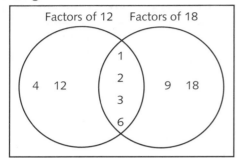

Factors of 12 · Factors of 18 · 4 · 12 · 1 · 2 · 3 · 6 · 9 · 18

2 1, 2, 4, 8
3 70
4 9

Challenge 3
1

×	5	8	9
4	20	32	36
6	30	48	54
12	60	96	108

2 3 or 9
3 1, 3, 7, 21
4 42

Pages 34–35
Challenge 1
1 **a)** 49 **b)** 36
   c) 25
2 **a)** 8 **b)** 27
   c) 64
3 26 is an even number. It can be divided by 2 and 13 as well as 1 and 26
4 **a)** $4^2 > 2^2$ **b)** $8^2 = 4^3$
   c) $3^3 > 5^2$

Challenge 2
1 **a)** 33 **b)** 24
   c) 41
2 ⑯⑨, ⑭④, ㊱, ㉕
3 **a)** $5^3 > 9^2$ **b)** $3^3 < 6^2$
   c) $7^2 < 4^3$

Challenge 3
1 **a)** 48 **b)** 49
2 $5 + 4 = 9$ or $7 + 9 = 16$

3
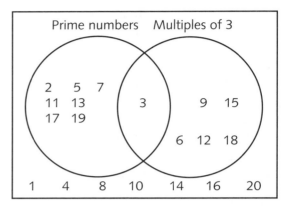

Prime numbers · Multiples of 3 · 2 · 5 · 7 · 11 · 13 · 17 · 19 · 3 · 9 · 15 · 6 · 12 · 18 · 1 · 4 · 8 · 10 · 14 · 16 · 20

4 ㊼, ㊾, ㊸

Pages 36–37
Challenge 1
1 32
2 **a)** 24.5 **b)** 510
   c) 1.56 **d)** 1600
3 **a)** 5.6 **b)** 13.56
   c) 340 **d)** 98
4 **a)** 90 **b)** 1500
   c) 60 **d)** 300
5 60p

Challenge 2
1 44
2 **a)** 543 **b)** 62
   c) 9.418 **d)** 24.6
3 **a)** 7291 **b)** 3.54
   c) 4.78 **d)** 5.69
4 **a)** 640 **b)** 600
   c) 60 **d)** 1800
5 12 tables

Challenge 3
1 **a)** 32
   b) 21
2 **a)** 675.4 **b)** 3.459
   c) 0.2415 **d)** 1300
3 10 bracelets
4 £38.40
5 Any pair of numbers from the following: 1,34; 2,68; 3,102; 4,136; 5,170... and so on

Pages 38–39
Challenge 1
1 805
2

×	**30**	3
50	1500	150
2	60	6

   1716
3 £11.16
4 715

Challenge 2

1

×	**400**	**70**	**3**
30	12 000	2100	90
6	2400	420	18

17 028

2 **a)** 888
b) 59.5

3 **a)** £21.96   **b)** £19.35

Challenge 3

1

2 £22.95

Pages 40–41
Challenge 1

1 **a)** 21   **b)** 16
c) 8.2

2 22 scouts

3 49 marbles

4 36 boxes

5 14 books

Challenge 2

1 **a)** 12   **b)** 17
c) 14.3

2 **a)** 80p   **b)** 22p
c) 26p   **d)** £1.28

3 16 presents

4 £7.15

Challenge 3

1 **a)** 17 beech trees
b) 7 apple trees, 14 pine trees
c) 24 lorry loads
d) £3.28

Pages 42–43
Challenge 1

1 **a)** 168   **b)** 832
c) 1032

2 **a)** 14   **b)** 18
c) 24   **d)** 17

Challenge 2

1 **a)** 75   **b)** 768
c) 888   **d)** 16 832

2 **a)** $15\frac{3}{6}$ or $15\frac{1}{2}$ **b)** $16\frac{3}{12}$ or $16\frac{1}{4}$
c) 27   **d)** 136

Challenge 3

1 **a)** 2183   **b)** 190
c) 38 428   **d)** 1086.24

2 **a)** 23   **b)** 15.5
c) 236   **d)** 24.15

Pages 44–45
Challenge 1

1 **a)** £2.73   **b)** 5 pencils
c) £8.16   **d)** 6 sharpeners

2 11 235p

3 14 seeds

Challenge 2

1 **a)** £88.80   **b)** 4 pairs
c) £29.45   **d)** 744 seeds

2 27p

3 £6.84

Challenge 3

1 **a)** £28.40
b) 12 adults
c) £171
d) Family tickets are cheaper.
Individual tickets = £18.80
e) 2 adult tickets and 3 student tickets

Pages 46–47
Challenge 1

1 Brackets, Order, Division, Multiplication,
Addition, Subtraction

2 3 + 4 x 2 = 11 ☐ ✓

3 **a)** 20   **b)** 21
c) 24   **d)** 12
e) 14   **f)** 5

Challenge 2

1 **a)** 21   **b)** 8
c) 36   **d)** 0
e) 35

2 James   26 − 3 + 2 x (4 + 3) ☐ ✓

Challenge 3

1 **a)** 35   **b)** 23

2 **a)** 2   **b)** 4
c) 4

3 $2^2 + 4 \times (5 + 7) \div 3 = 20$

Pages 48–49
Challenge 1

1 **a)** Any 1 square   **b)** Any 1 square
c) Any 3 squares

2 **a)** $\frac{4}{5}$ **b)** $\frac{1}{4}$
c) $\frac{1}{3}$

3 **a)** Any 2 squares   **b)** Any 1 square
c) Any 4 squares

Answers

Challenge 2

1. a) $\frac{3}{10}$ b) $\frac{1}{6}$
   c) $\frac{2}{8}$ or $\frac{1}{4}$ d) $\frac{2}{9}$

2. a) $\frac{1}{4}$ b) $\frac{3}{4}$
   c) $\frac{2}{11}$

3. Any 9 marbles shaded

4. a) $\frac{3}{4} = \frac{6}{8}$ b) $\frac{1}{3} < \frac{10}{15}$
   c) $\frac{5}{12} < \frac{4}{8}$

Challenge 3

1. a) 6 boxes shaded black, 9 boxes shaded green, 4 boxes shaded blue, 5 boxes left white
   b) Black: 6, Green: 9, Blue: 4, White: 5

2.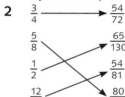

Pages 50–51
Challenge 1

1. a) 3 chickens shaded black, 2 chickens shaded brown, 7 chickens left white
   b) Black 3, Brown 2, White 7

2. a) 4   b) 3
   c) 5

3. a) 3   b) 8
   c) 20

4. a) 2   b) 10
   c) 9

5. 6 marbles

Challenge 2

1. a) 5 squares shaded yellow, 2 squares shaded purple, 8 squares shaded green, 1 square shaded red
   b) Yellow: 5, Purple: 2, Green: 8, Red: 1
   c) $\frac{4}{20}$ or $\frac{1}{5}$

2. a) 18   b) 9
   c) 27

3. a) 16   b) 80
   c) 48

4. a) 20   b) 45
   c) 60

5. 42 beads

Challenge 3

1. a) 10 squares shaded orange, 20 squares shaded blue, 25 squares shaded pink, 15 squares shaded grey, 16 squares shaded green
   b) Orange: 10, Blue: 20, Pink: 25, Grey: 15, Green: 16
   c) 14 squares
   d) $\frac{14}{100}$ or $\frac{7}{50}$

2. a) $\frac{4}{5}$ b) 6
   c) 30

Pages 52–53
Challenge 1

1. a) $\frac{1}{4} + \frac{1}{4} = \frac{2}{4}$ or $\frac{1}{2}$ b) $\frac{5}{6} + \frac{1}{6} = \frac{6}{6}$ or 1 whole

2. a) $\frac{6}{7}$ b) $\frac{8}{12}$ (or $\frac{2}{3}$)
   c) $\frac{3}{5}$

3. a) $\frac{4}{15}$ b) $\frac{1}{12}$
   c) $\frac{9}{10}$

Challenge 2

1. a) $\frac{1}{4} + \frac{1}{8} = \frac{3}{8}$ b) $\frac{1}{2} + \frac{3}{8} = \frac{7}{8}$

2. a) $\frac{7}{10}$ b) $\frac{3}{4}$
   c) $\frac{5}{8}$

3. a) $\frac{3}{10}$ b) $\frac{8}{12}$ (or $\frac{2}{3}$)
   c) $\frac{1}{4}$

Challenge 3

1. a) $\frac{1}{4} + \frac{1}{6} = \frac{5}{12}$ b) $\frac{3}{6} - \frac{1}{4} = \frac{3}{12}$ or $\frac{1}{4}$

2. a) $\frac{5}{12}$ b) $\frac{13}{12}$
   c) $\frac{19}{21}$

3. a) $\frac{4}{15}$ b) $\frac{5}{12}$
   c) $\frac{9}{20}$

Pages 54–55
Challenge 1

1. a) $\frac{1}{6}$ b) $\frac{1}{2}$
   c) $\frac{1}{4}$ d) $\frac{1}{4}$

2. a) $\frac{1}{15}$ b) $\frac{1}{18}$
   c) $\frac{1}{8}$

3. a) $\frac{1}{4}$ b) $\frac{1}{8}$
   c) $\frac{1}{6}$

Challenge 2

1. a) $\frac{1}{18}$ b) $\frac{1}{4}$
   c) $\frac{1}{16}$ d) $\frac{1}{21}$

Answers

2 **a)** $\frac{1}{36}$ **b)** $\frac{1}{28}$

c) $\frac{1}{72}$

3 **a)** $\frac{1}{16}$ **b)** $\frac{1}{40}$

c) $\frac{1}{30}$

Challenge 3

1 **a)** $\frac{1}{72}$ **b)** $\frac{1}{16}$

c) Any two appropriate fractions.
For example: $\frac{1}{4}$ and $\frac{1}{2}$

d) Any two appropriate fractions.
For example: $\frac{1}{10}$ and $\frac{1}{5}$

2 **a)** $\frac{1}{63}$ **b)** $\frac{1}{45}$

c) $\frac{1}{60}$ **d)** $\frac{1}{40}$

e) $\frac{1}{100}$ **f)** $\frac{1}{72}$

3 **a)** $\frac{1}{16}$ **b)** $\frac{1}{30}$

c) $\frac{1}{40}$ **d)** $\frac{1}{100}$

e) $\frac{1}{144}$ **f)** $\frac{1}{256}$

Pages 56–57
Challenge 1

1 **a)** 0.5 **b)** 0.75

c) 0.25

2 **a)** 3.5 **b)** 0.58

3 A = 0.2, B = 0.5, C = 0.9

4 **a)** 33 **b)** 169

c) 1

Challenge 2

1 **a)** 1.5 **b)** 0.01

c) 0.125

2 A = 0.05, B = 0.30, C = 0.45

3 **a)** 0.342 **b)** 105

c) 0.2456

4 **a)** 38.6 **b)** 147.3

c) 2.9

Challenge 3

1 **a)** 0.035 **b)** 1.125

c) 0.0625

2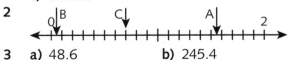

3 **a)** 48.6 **b)** 245.4

c) 7.0

4

Pages 58–59
Challenge 1

1 **a)** $1\frac{1}{4}$ **b)** $2\frac{1}{2}$

c) $1\frac{3}{4}$ **d)** $3\frac{1}{4}$

2 **b)** $\frac{5}{2}$

c) $\frac{7}{4}$ **d)** $\frac{13}{4}$

3 **a)** $\frac{4}{3}$ **b)** $\frac{7}{5}$

c) $\frac{3}{2}$

4 $\frac{7}{6}, \frac{10}{4}$

Challenge 2

1 **a)** 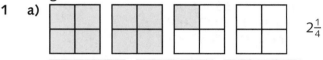 $2\frac{1}{4}$

b) 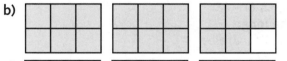 $2\frac{5}{6}$

c)  $1\frac{2}{3}$

d) 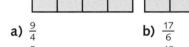 $1\frac{5}{8}$

2 **a)** $\frac{9}{4}$ **b)** $\frac{17}{6}$

c) $\frac{5}{3}$ **d)** $\frac{13}{8}$

3 **a)** $1\frac{3}{6}$ or $1\frac{1}{2}$ **b)** $5\frac{1}{3}$

c) $2\frac{3}{4}$

4 **a)** $\frac{9}{5}$ **b)** $\frac{11}{8}$

c) $\frac{6}{5}$

Challenge 3

1 **a)** $2\frac{1}{3}$ **b)** $1\frac{1}{8}$

2 **a)** $1\frac{1}{5}$ **b)** $1\frac{1}{4}$

3

4 **a)** $\frac{15}{12} < \frac{9}{6}$ **b)** $\frac{5}{2} > \frac{7}{6}$

c) $1\frac{1}{4} < \frac{11}{8}$

Pages 60–61
Challenge 1

1 **a)** 100% **b)** 75%

c) 50% **d)** 25%

2 **a)** 8 **b)** 32

c) 30 **d)** 40

Answers

3 **a)** Training top = £45
   b) Ball = £15
   c) Gloves = £9
Challenge 2
1 **a)** £13.50   **b)** 54
   c) 64   **d)** 48
2 **a)** 40%   **b)** 24%
   c) 20%   **d)** 25%
3 **a)** Skirt = £16.80
   b) Trousers = £35.70
   c) T-shirt = £19.25
Challenge 3
1 Geography
2 **House A** £368000
   House B £977500
   House C £745200

Pages 62–63
Challenge 1
1 12 marbles
2 £7.40
3 **a)** 0.8   **b)** 0.04
   c) 0.75
4 Any 3 squares shaded
5 25p, 250p, £2.53, £25
Challenge 2
1 **a)** Dogs: 40 children, Cats: 100 children,
   Rabbits: 240 children, Goldfish: 20 children
   b) 60 children
2 **a)** 45 cows   **b)** $\frac{1}{2}$
3 Any 12 triangles shaded
Challenge 3
1 **a)** 60   **b)** 39
2

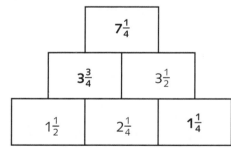

Pages 64–67
Progress Test 2
1 $\frac{1}{24}$
2 ㊲ ㊳ ㊲ ㊲ (37, 53, 67, 97)
3 $\frac{1}{20}$ or $\frac{5}{100}$
4 159.24

5

×	5	6	9
7	**35**	42	**63**
8	**40**	**48**	72
6	**30**	**36**	**54**

6 $\frac{13}{5}$
7 120
8 16, 25, 64
9 **a)** 0.35   **b)** 0.9
   c) 0.4
10 28 boxes
11 $4\frac{4}{5}$
12 16
13 $26\frac{2}{5}$
14 1, 36, 2, 18, 3, 12, 4, 9, 6
15 £21.25
16 1645
17 109
18 **a)** £38.96   **b)** £19.48
19 £468.75
20 $\frac{1}{18}$
21 76 cards
22 16°C
23 2004
24 130
25 **a)** 40000
   b) 42700
   c) 43000
26 86.44 km
27 1003, 1104, 1205
28 433 ml

Pages 68–69
Challenge 1
1 **a)** 2 hearts : 3 clubs
   b) 2 hearts : 1 club
   c) 4 hearts : 4 clubs, or 1 heart : 1 club
2 ○●●●●○●●●●○●●●
3 **a)** 1:3   **b)** 1:2
   c) 1:8   **d)** 1:4
Challenge 2
1 **a)** 1 heart and 3 clubs drawn
   b) 2 hearts and 4 clubs drawn
   c) 4 hearts and 3 clubs drawn
2 No. I would need 12 red beads to use up all
   18 blue beads.
3 **a)** £1.20   **b)** 300 g

Answers

Challenge 3
1   Parcel 250 g Letter 50 g
2   **a)** 27 blue marbles
    b) Blue: 36   Green: 60

Pages 70–71
Challenge 1
1   26 cm
2   9 times longer
Challenge 2
1
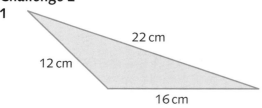

Challenge 3
1   7 times larger
2   **a)** 0.3 m   **b)** 0.1 m
    c) 0.04 m
3   B is 11 times bigger
    C is 3.5 times bigger

Pages 72–73
Challenge 1
1

Sunflowers	Beans
1	3
2	**6**
5	**15**
10	**30**

2

	For 4 people	For 8 people
Apples	100 g	**200 g**
Grapes	120 g	**240 g**
Oranges	40 g	**80 g**

Challenge 2
1

	For 12 people	For 4 people
Beef	480 g	**160 g**
Potatoes	270 g	**90 g**
Carrots	150 g	**50 g**
White sauce	210 ml	**70 ml**

2   9 cups

Challenge 3
1

	For 4 people	For 6 people
Oats	248 g	**372 g**
Butter	320 g	**480 g**
Syrup	124 ml	**186 ml**
Sultanas	96 g	**144 g**

2   Mango juice: 300 ml, orange juice: 450 ml, sparkling water: 750 ml

Pages 74–75
Challenge 1
1   **a)** $x = 6$ **b)** $y = 23$
    c) $x = 7$
2   **a)** 22   **b)** 5
3

n	$4n - 2$
1	2
5	**18**
10	**38**
20	**78**
100	**398**

Challenge 2
1   **a)** $x = 5$ **b)** $y = 3$
2   1 and 15, 3 and 5
3   **a)** 33   **b)** 95
4   $a = 14, b = 8$
Challenge 3
1   $a = 7$
2   1 and 32, 2 and 16, 4 and 8
3

n	$3n - 5$	n^2	$100n$
7	**16**	**49**	**700**
8	**19**	64	**800**
12	31	**144**	**1200**
45	**130**	**2025**	4500

Pages 76–77
Challenge 1
1   4, 8, 12, **16, 20, 24**
2   310
3   Add 4 each time
Challenge 2
1   Add 8 each time
2   24, 15, 6, **–3, –12, –21**
3   **27**, 36, 45, **54**, 63
Challenge 3
1   Add a squared number each time
2   23, 31.5, 40, **48.5, 57, 65.5**
3   56, **63, 70, 77**, 84

121

Answers

4 **a)** $3n + 1$

b)

Term (n)	1	2	3	10	100
Number	4	7	10	**31**	**301**

Pages 78–79
Challenge 1
1 4.30pm
2 **a)** 1 m **b)** 5.5 kg
   c) 50 mm **d)** 3 minutes
3 850 ml
Challenge 2
1

mm	cm	m	km
39000	**3900**	39	**0.039**
45	**4.5**	0.045	0.000045
1430000	**143000**	**1430**	1.43
2670	267	**2.67**	0.00267

2 **a)** 650 ml **b)** 350 ml
3 230 seconds
Challenge 3
1 James
2 15 cm
3 150 g
4 40 days

Pages 80–81
Challenge 1
1 P = 24 m
2 P = 10 m A = 6 m²
3 A = 15 m²
Challenge 2
1 P = 40 cm
2 A = 176 m²
3 A = 7 cm²
Challenge 3
1 **a)** 40 m **b)** 71 m²
2 Any suitable answer, e.g.

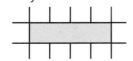

Pages 82–83
Challenge 1
1 V = 64 cm³
2 A = 30 cm²
Challenge 2
1 A = 96 cm²
2 Sail A = 6 m², Sail B = 14 m²
3 4 cm
Challenge 3
1 A = 58.5 cm²
2 V = 3000 cm³

Pages 84–87
Progress Test 3
1 **a)** 1 pint **b)** 35 cm **c)** 1 mile
2 V = 105 cm³
3 **a)** 6 bananas, 18 oranges
   b) 26 mangoes, 13 bananas, 39 oranges
4 10 cups
5 1 and 6 or 2 and 3
6 7, 11.5, 16, **20.5**, **25**, **29.5**
7 A = 27 m²
8 21st June
9 Red = 45, Green = 30, White = 60
10 2 hours and 40 minutes
11 851 m
12 52 cm
13 $\frac{6}{7}$
14 20%
15 400
16

3^2	4^3	3^3	9^2	5^3
9	**64**	27	**81**	125

17 35
18 32.43, 33.34, 33.4, 33.43, 34.04
19 –111, –77
20 62 367 and 512 356
21 –5°C
22 **a)** 615 380
   b) 615 000
   c) 615 400
   d) 620 000
23 **a)** 53
   b) 89
   c) 14
24 **a)** £31.85
   b) Swimming costume and snorkel set
   c) £49.84

Pages 88–89
Challenge 1
1

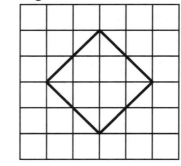

2 It has two equal sides. ✓

Its angles all add up to 180°. ✓

Challenge 2
1 $x = 79°$

2
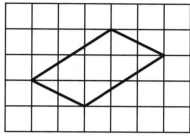

Challenge 3
1
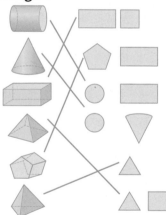

Accept similar shape with 4 sides and only one pair of parallel sides.

2 **a)** D
 b) A, B, C, D
 c) B, D
 d) A, C

Pages 90–91
Challenge 1
1
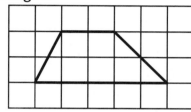

2 Faces: 5, Edges: 8, Vertices: 5

Challenge 2
1

2 Faces: 7, Edges: 15, Vertices: 10
3 Cuboid

Challenge 3
1 Faces: 6, Edges: 9, Vertices: 5

2
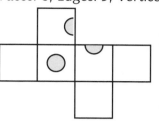

Pages 92–93
Challenge 1
1 8 cm
2 6 m
3 24 cm

Challenge 2
1 1.25 m
2 10 beads
3 Radius = 25 cm   Diameter = 50 cm

Challenge 3
1 23 cm
2 0.95 cm
3 7 cm ✓

Pages 94–95
Challenge 1
1 **a)** $x = 25°$ **b)** $x = 45°$
 c) $x = 125°$
2 $x = 40°$ Accept 38° to 42°
3 $x = 125°$

Challenge 2
1 50°
2 **a)** $x = 107°$ **b)** $x = 29°$
 c) $x = 263°$

Challenge 3
1 **a)** $x = 72°$ $y = 108°$
 b) $x = 68°$ $y = 67°$

Pages 96–97
Challenge 1
1 **a)**
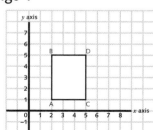

 b) Rectangle
 c) (2,3)

Answers

Challenge 2

1 a)

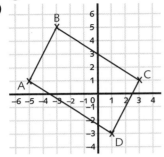

b) Parallelogram **c)** (–2, –1)

Challenge 3

1 a) and **b)**, and **d)**.

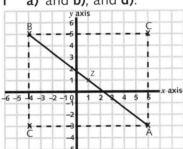

c) (1,1)
e) (6,5) or (–4, –3)

Pages 98–99
Challenge 1

1 a) (–3,3), (–1,3), (–1,5), (–3,5)

b)

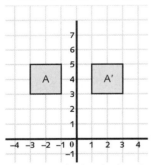

c) (1,3), (3,3), (1,5), (3,5)

Challenge 2

1 a) (–5,2), (–3,2), (–3,4), (–5,4)

b)

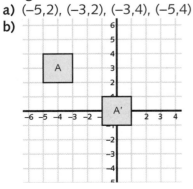

c) (1,1), (1,–1), (–1,1), (–1,–1)

Challenge 3

1 a) (–6,1), (–3,1), (–2,4), (–5,4)

b)

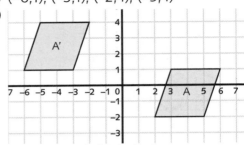

c) (2,–2), (5,–2), (6,1), (3,1)

Pages 100–101
Challenge 1

1 a) (–3,2), (–4,2), (–3,5), (–4,5)

b)

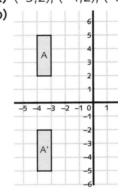

c) (–3,–2), (–4,–2), (–3,–5), (–4,–5)

Challenge 2

1 a) (1,3), (4,4), (1,5)

b)

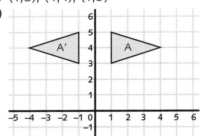

c) (–1,3), (–4,4), (–1,5)

Challenge 3

1 a)

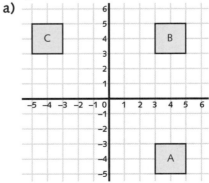

b) Shape A (5,–3), (3,–3), (5,–5), (3,–5)
Shape B (5,3), (3,3), (5,5), (3,5)

Pages 102–103
Challenge 1
1 **a)** Degrees Celsius (°C)
  b) 10 am   **c)** 18°C
  d) 2 pm   **e)** 10°C

Challenge 2
1 **a)** 14°C
  b) 13 recordings
  c) 1 pm and 3 pm
  d) 1 pm & 3 pm and 11am & 7pm
  e) 0°C

Challenge 3
1 **a)** 15°C
  b) 9
  c) 20°C
  d) 10 am   8 pm   9 pm   10 pm
  e) 10°C

Pages 104–105
Challenge 1
1 **a)** Piano   **b)** Recorder
  c) $\frac{1}{2}$ **d)** 30 children
  e) 9 Accept 8 or 10

Challenge 2
1 **a)** $\frac{4}{15}$ **b)** 16 children Accept 17
  c) 25 children

2 Key
  Apple
  Orange
  Banana

Challenge 3
1

Favourite pet	Number	%	Degrees / 360
Cat	100	50	180
Stick insect	10	5	18
Budgie	40	20	72
Dog	50	25	90
Total	200	100	360

2

  Key
  ▨ Cat
  ⋮ Stick Insect
  ☐ Budgie
  ▦ Dog

Pages 106–107
Challenge 1
1 6   2 10 sweets
3 25p   4 4 goals

Challenge 2
1 150 g   2 10
3 145 cm

Challenge 3
1 340 cm   2 14 mugs
3 £4.33

Pages 108–111
Progress Test 4
1 **a)** 8 students   **b)** $\frac{2}{32}$ Accept $\frac{1}{16}$
  c) 4 students
2 Triangular-based prism
3 13
4 (4, –3)
5 $x = 58°$
6 9 cm
7 **a)** 60 miles
  b) 8 gallons
  c) 330 miles Accept 325–335 miles
  d) 9 gallons
  e) 105 miles Accept 101–110 miles
8 $\frac{15}{16}$
9 Blue = 25%, Red = 50%, Black = 12.5%, Green = 12.5%
10 36 cm
11 $x = 6$
12 **a)** A = 8 cm²
  b) P = 16 cm
13

	12 people	3 people
Pasta	200 g	50 g
Ham	96 g	24 g
Cheese	120 g	30 g
Cream	180 ml	45 ml

14 7
15 19
16 9000 cm³
17 1.05 pm
18 3600
19 **a)** 60   **b)** 446
20 £1.13
21 **a)** 12   **b)** 86
  c) 37
22 **a)** –6°C, 40°C   **b)** 46°C

Progress Test Charts

Progress Test 1

Q	Topic	✓ or X	See page
1	Negative Numbers		14
2	Place Value		12
3	Written Addition and Subtraction		22
4	Mental Calculations		20
5	Mental Calculations		20
6	Written Addition and Subtraction		22
7	Mental Calculations		20
8	Mental Calculations		20
9	Place Value		12
10	Addition and Subtraction Practice		24
11	Place Value		12
12	Mental Calculations		20
13	Mental Calculations		20
14	Written Addition and Subtraction		22
15	Mental Calculations		20
16	Written Addition and Subtraction		22
17	Mental Calculations		20
18	Place Value		12
19	Multistep Problems		26
20	Place Value		12
21	Mental Calculations		20
22	Mental Calculations		20
23	Mental Calculations		20
24	Place Value		12
25	Written Addition and Subtraction		22
26	Rounding		16
27	Addition and Subtraction Practice		24
28	Addition and Subtraction Practice		24
29	Negative Numbers		14
30	Rounding		16

Progress Test 2

Q	Topic	✓ or X	See page
1	Multiplying and Dividing Fractions		54
2	Prime, Square and Cube Numbers		34
3	Adding and Subtracting Fractions		52
4	Written Multiplication		38
5	Factors and Multiples		32
6	Improper Fractions and Mixed Numbers		58
7	Percentages		60
8	Prime, Square and Cube Numbers		34
9	Decimal Fractions		56
10	Multiplying and Dividing		36
11	Improper Fractions and Mixed Numbers		58
12	BODMAS		46
13	Written Short and Long Division		40
14	Factors and Multiples		32
15	Percentages		60
16	Written Multiplication		38
17	Prime, Square and Cube Numbers		34
18	Written Multiplication		38
19	Written Multiplication		38
20	Multiplying and Dividing Fractions		54
21	Multiplying and Dividing		36
22	Negative Numbers		14
23	Mental Calculations		20
24	Mental Calculations		20
25	Rounding		16
26	Written Addition and Subtraction		22
27	Place Value		12
28	Mental Calculations		20

Progress Test 3

Q	Topic	✓ or ✗	See page
1	Units of Measurement		78
2	Area of Triangles and Parallelograms and Volume of Shapes		82
3	Ratio		68
4	Units of Measurement		78
5	Formulae and Equations		74
6	Linear Number Sequences		76
7	Perimeter and Area		80
8	Mental Calculations		20
9	Ratio		68
10	Units of Measurement		78
11	Units of Measurement		78
12	Perimeter and Area		80
13	Adding and Subtracting Fractions		52
14	Percentages		60
15	Multiplying and Dividing		36
16	Prime, Square and Cube Numbers		34
17	Multiplying and Dividing		36
18	Place Value		12
19	Linear Number Sequences		76
20	Place Value		12
21	Negative Numbers		14
22	Rounding		16
23	Mental Calculations		36
24	Written Addition and Subtraction		22

Progress Test 4

Q	Topic	✓ or ✗	See page
1	Pie Charts		104
2	3-D Shapes and Nets		90
3	Calculating Mean		106
4	Coordinates		96
5	Missing Angles		94
6	Circles		92
7	Line Graphs		102
8	Adding and Subtracting Fractions		52
9	Percentages		60
10	Scale Factor		70
11	Formulae and Equations		74
12	Perimeter and Area		80
13	Ratio		68
14	Formulae and Equations		74
15	Linear Number Sequences		76
16	Area of Triangles and Parallelograms and Volume of Shapes		82
17	Units of Measurement		78
18	Rounding		16
19	Mental Calculations		20
20	Written Addition and Subtraction		22
21	Mental Calculations		20
22	Negative Numbers		14

What am I doing well in? _____

_____

What do I need to improve? _____

_____

Notes